WHAT OTHERS SA
THE WILDS OF ...

For many years Rick Lamplugh has passionately engaged the wild world—trekking remote wilderness, bicycling roads less traveled, and advocating for wolves. In *The Wilds of Aging,* Lamplugh turns to the privacy of his small garden to negotiate the inner wilderness of his own mortality. In outwardly flowing meditations that are as clear and honest as a mountain stream, he delves into the deepest canyons of his being: loss of family and friends, a dysfunctional father, his own inevitable physical decline and death, even a possible afterlife. On this journey, Lamplugh charts his own course. Yet as you travel with him you will begin to notice familiar looking terrain. Eventually, you'll round a corner in the trail and find that you are suddenly face to face—with yourself.

TOM A. TITUS
author of *Blackberries in July: A Forager's Field Guide to Inner Peace*

Rick Lamplugh explores his own aging, and all that portends for him, with the spirit of a true adventurer. The stories that ensue brim with heart and curiosity. His genius is to make us feel all the more alive in the presence of our mortality. In navigating my wild elder years, I could ask for no better guide.

MARY REYNOLDS THOMPSON
author of *Reclaiming the Wild Soul:
How Earth's Landscapes Restore Us to Wholeness*

Piercing and poetic, Rick Lamplugh turns his love for wild places and an adventurer's heart toward a new, interior landscape. Exploring the vulnerabilities and the exaltations of being human, *The Wilds of Aging* maps a scenic route through this universal wilderness, creating a tender, resonant tale of transcendence and transformation.

CAROLINE KRAUS
founder, Moments of Truth Project

Baby Boomers who dread aging can take heart from the example of Rick Lamplugh, who spent a year in his garden facing big questions and big fears about declining physical abilities and death and emerged ready to begin a meaningful new chapter of his life. In a kind of prequel to his two highly acclaimed Yellowstone books, *The Wilds of Aging* traces the journey of heart and mind that finally opened Lamplugh to becoming an advocate for wildlife and wild lands.

LORRAINE ANDERSON
editor of *Sisters of the Earth* and *Earth & Eros*

Rick Lamplugh wrestles with accepting declining physical abilities and facing his mortality. He agonizes for an answer to the insoluble question: What happens after death? A new life? Nothingness? You are at his side as he explores the wilds of aging.

DICK WEINMAN
author of *Two Different Worlds*

After all the adventuring through the world at large, the one great uncharted wilderness we are still faced with is our own journey toward death. Rick Lamplugh has blazed an insightful and heartfelt trail into "the wilds of aging." We would do well to lace up our boots and follow it.

MARC BEAUDIN
author of *Vagabond Song: Neo-Haibun from the Peregrine Journals*

The death of friends as we ease into elderhood makes us think about our mortality, and Rick Lamplugh has discovered it's time to grapple with that inevitability. With his garden as touchstone and his spouse and friends as chorus, in *The Wilds of Aging* he contemplates with honesty and integrity his future as an aging adventurer.

STEPHEN TRIMBLE
author of *Bargaining for Eden*
and co-author of *The Geography of Childhood:
Why Children Need Wild Places*

Rick Lamplugh's book offers a fascinating look into one man's coming to terms with his own aging process. Through narrative contemplations of his many friends' experiences, his complex relationship with his father, and his journeys as an adventurer, Rick sheds light on how a person can be not just an observer of the aging process, but an active and engaged participant.

ANN MCQUEEN, PH.D.

The Wilds of Aging provides some important takeaways: live every moment to the fullest, find the things and people you are passionate about and focus on them, and aging does not mean the end of enjoying life--aging might cause you to appreciate life more fully.

LORI SMETANKA
executive director,
The National Consumer Voice for Quality Long Term Care

Rick beautifully weaves a deep love of the outdoors and nature into a poignant and tangible contemplation of aging. A wonderful and moving read.

JENNY GOLDING
editor, *AYellowstoneLife.com*

Also by Rick Lamplugh

In the Temple of Wolves:
A Winter's Immersion in Wild Yellowstone

Deep into Yellowstone:
A Year's Immersion in Grandeur and Controversy

The Wilds of Aging

A Journey of Heart and Mind

Rick Lamplugh

The Wilds of Aging text © 2018 by Rick Lamplugh

Photo of author © 2018 by Mary Strickroth

Cover and interior design: Open Heart Designs

Catalog information: The Wilds of Aging: A Journey of Heart and Mind / Rick Lamplugh. —1st edition.

1. Aging—Religious Aspects
2. Aging—Social Aspects
3. Aging—Psychological Aspects
4. Lamplugh, Rick—Journeys
5. Lamplugh, Rick, 1948-

ISBN-13: 978-1727310344
ISBN-10: 1727310349

Printed in the United States of America on library-quality stock

10 9 8 7 6 5 4 3 2 1

For Mary, Allison, Lapaka, Zack, Hana, and Siena

Contents

A Note from the Author

Many readers of my two books about Yellowstone have asked me how I came to center my life around the park's wildlife and wild lands. How I came to live in Gardiner, Montana, at the park's north gate.

I usually tell the short story. Once we retired, Mary and I decided to live and volunteer for three winters at the Lamar Buffalo Ranch in Yellowstone's Lamar Valley, wolf central for the park. That experience led to my writing *In the Temple of Wolves: A Winter's Immersion in Wild Yellowstone*. That immersion changed our lives, opening our hearts and minds to what we were missing by staying in Corvallis, Oregon, where we had lived for thirty-five years. Though we couldn't imagine moving at first, we eventually accepted the pull of Yellowstone and relocated to Gardiner. Once here, we found plenty of grandeur, but as we settled in we found that Gardiner sits at the center of a number of controversies. That led to my writing *Deep into Yellowstone: A Year's Immersion in Grandeur and Controversy*.

But there's more to this tale. *The Wilds of Aging: A Journey of Heart and Mind* reveals the rest. I wrote what would become the first draft of this book three years before we volunteered at the Buffalo Ranch, years before we moved to Gardiner, and I dove deeply into advocating for wildlife and wild lands.

I had no intention of publishing that first draft, which was my journaling during a year I spent exploring aging, declining physical abilities, my mortality, and what might happen when I die. That journaling was a yearlong visit to a "paper therapist."

When the year ended, I put the journal away; the writing had served its purpose. I was ready to adventure again, and soon Yellowstone, Gardiner, and advocating called.

But recently, after having helped another loved one through her final months, and after getting even older, I pulled out that journal again. I read it and realized with a shock that here was the long, painful process that had opened me to that life-changing experience of volunteering and living in the Lamar Valley. Here was how I came to understand that if there was something I felt drawn to do in my remaining years, I had better do it.

I know I'm not alone in dreading the physical, mental, and emotional changes aging brings. Every day, many others feel a pang of aging: a new ache, a struggle to remember, the pain of peers passing away. These pangs can be denied or ignored, as I did for so long. But eventually the big questions, big doubts, and big fears demand to be faced. It took me a year in the garden to face mine.

I hope you enjoy this adventurous journey of heart and mind.

CHAPTER 1

The North Cascades

WITHOUT EXPECTING TO, I BEGAN MY JOURNEY INTO THE wilds of aging during a two-week-long, 375-mile bicycle tour at age sixty. I rode alone, lugging a fifty-pound trailer stuffed with camping gear up and down the mountains of Washington's North Cascades in July.

I don't usually tour alone, but one of my riding partners, my wife, Mary, had to work. My other riding partner, Jim, had to drop out just after he and I had finished making the plans and preparations for the tour. I decided to go solo, even though doing so made me nervous: I would have no one with whom to share the daily challenges of a long ride in mountainous, unfamiliar territory, no one to encourage or be encouraged by.

But the challenges of this long tour also excited me. I enjoy adventuring and pushing myself. During each of the seven previous summers, Mary and I had completed weeks-long adventures—biking or hiking—that we designed to stretch ourselves physically, mentally, and emotionally. We pedaled long, self-supported bike rides in mountains and deserts in our home state of Oregon. We hiked deep into the wild backcountry of Yellowstone and Glacier national parks. We struggled side by side up mountains in the West and in Maine.

So there I was, halfway into the North Cascades tour, alone and cooking in full sun as I cycled up a steep road in a canyon scented by the hot lodgepole pines that dotted its sunbaked walls. Occasionally, a few pines shaded the road, but I passed through the shade far too quickly. The temperature broke ninety degrees before noon. The air rising from the blacktop was surely hotter.

The grade showed no sign of ending, and that oven of a road was challenging me like nothing had before. Even though I alternated standing and sitting as I pedaled, my legs grew limp and my pedaling slowed. But I kept pushing—and nervously glancing at the heart rate monitor on my sports watch. As the beats-per-minute number climbed, I fantasized the monitor would soon flash 9-1-1. And I was way out of cell phone range.

As the day burned on, the distance between breaks grew shorter. Each time I stopped, I forced myself to drink the now-hot—not just warm—water I carried. Finally, I heard the call of rushing water and pulled off the road.

I dismounted and picked my way rock by rock down a steep bank to an enticing stream. I knelt, dunked my head completely into the cold water, and kept it there until I ran out of air. I jerked my head out of the water and shook it like a wet dog would. Gasping, I lay back on a hot rock and proclaimed to the empty sky, "That's it. I've hit my limit." The confession surprised me: that was the first time I had ever admitted reaching a physical limit.

I wanted to believe that the problem was just the hill, the heat, the hour, nothing I couldn't overcome. But lying there, feeling the sun vaporize water off my face, I wasn't so sure. I even wondered if pushing on might be dangerous. What if I passed out while cycling alone on this little-used mountain road?

Still, I had miles to go before making camp, and introspection—or lying on that rock and drinking that stream dry—wouldn't get me there. I stripped off my sweat-stained, yellow biking shirt and submerged it in the creek. Not bothering to wring it out, I pulled it on and shivered as if I had just jumped into the stream.

I climbed up the bank to my bike and looked ahead. I faced many switchbacks; each would bring me closer to my next goal, mile-high Washington Pass, up there in the conifers and flanked by ragged mountain peaks. I shook my head at the elevation and distance yet to cover. Then I mounted up, gritted my teeth, and pedaled on.

I made it to the pass and down the other side, and eventually reached camp. When I finally stepped off my bike, I stumbled, exhausted, to the site's picnic table. I looked at the fire pit but knew there would be no campfire for me. I would just eat, set up my tent, and lay my tired old body down.

Several days later I finished the tour, but the memory of reaching my limit that day stuck in my craw. Once back home, I told Jim, who is four years older than I, and Mary, who is four years younger, how I had reached my limit and how much that bothered me. They both said I'd get over it.

That sounded good. But I doubted it.

CHAPTER 2

South Sister

A MONTH AFTER THAT SOLO BIKE TOUR, MARY AND I stepped out of our tent at three in the morning to start a climb of 10,358-foot South Sister in Oregon's Cascades. We chattered with energy and excitement, awed by the otherworldly glow of our headlamps' beams glittering off a white gravel trail. We weren't expecting a tough hike; this route is a "walk-up" that thousands of people attempt each year, and most make it. We were climbing as a warm-up for a higher—and more challenging—peak in Wyoming later in the summer.

As the day wore on and we climbed above tree line, my energy and excitement wore out. I struggled on in fits and starts, heart pounding, thighs burning. My breaks grew longer and more frequent, just as they had in the North Cascades.

On one break, I turned and gazed downhill. Below me, Mary moved slowly but steadily up the mountain in what she calls "chug mode." Watching her patient progress, I caught myself trying to convince myself that I had gone far enough. That the smart move was to quit pushing, turn around, and cruise downhill. That I had nothing to prove. That I wasn't a failure.

I shook off these thoughts and moved on. Rounding a corner, I came upon the start of a mile-long steeper section of loose, rough, red volcanic rock that we would have to slip and slide up to reach the now-visible summit. Two young men sat comfortably beside the trail.

I stopped and asked, "Are you going for the summit?"

One of the young men, hood up, arms across his chest, shook his head and answered, "No, I'm not going any farther."

Projecting that he might be struggling, as I was, with feeling like a failure, I encouraged him to go on.

There was a moment of silence and then the second young man looked at me, smiled, and said, "I've never climbed a mountain before, and I'm happy to have gotten this high. I think I'll stop right here too."

I glanced down the trail and saw Mary, still out of earshot. I turned to the young men and complimented them on knowing their limits. Then I said, "I don't know how many more mountains I have inside me." I felt surprised at telling two strangers something I had never told anyone, not even myself. They nodded silently. I nodded back.

I walked ahead a few paces and waited for Mary. Together, she and I climbed on, challenging and encouraging one another as we had done on so many other hikes.

When we finally stepped hand in hand onto the summit of South Sister, I knew—as I had on that solo bike tour—that I had reached a physical limit. As I gazed down the mountain to where the young men had accepted their limits, reaching this summit felt like senseless suffering, not the grand accomplishment I had hoped for.

After slogging back to base camp, Mary and I sat on a fallen log and watched late afternoon thunderheads form. As the clouds rumbled our way, we retreated to the tent. While Mary napped, I lay on my back, tired but unable to sleep. Hands locked behind my head, I stared at the tent ceiling. I thought about my last two outings—one solo, one not—and how I had reached the limit of my endurance and questioned the value of pushing on.

Lightning cracked, thunder boomed, and the mountains echoed. I curled up into the protection of my sleeping bag and realized there was more: I had confessed to the young men that I didn't know how many more mountains I could tackle. That statement revealed something that should have been obvious long ago: aging and declining physical abilities could kill the adventuring I so loved. Worse yet, aging would eventually kill me.

I watched drops of rain land on the tent fly, join into rivulets, and slide downward, pushing dust ahead. Of course I was aging; everyone ages—if they're lucky. And everyone dies—lucky or not. The real wonder was that I had denied these ancient and obvious truths for so long. How had I managed to maintain, like Peter Pan, an illusion of unending youth?

CHAPTER 3

The Wall

PRESERVING THAT ILLUSION HAD REQUIRED ME TO BUILD a wall around myself, a wall that blocked thoughts of my mortality, a wall so strong that even at sixty years of age I had not accepted the reality of aging. But that South Sister climb and the North Cascades bike tour had proved to me that regardless of what I'm willing to admit, my body is aging, and aging leads to physical decline and eventually death.

I started building that protective wall a decade earlier when Jana, our friend of eighteen years, died from cancer. She was younger than me and my equal in the way she challenged and cared for her athletic body. If she couldn't beat death, I wondered then, how could I? That glimpse of a terrible truth threatened my illusion of unending youth. I mixed a big batch of denial and started building. The wall wasn't big or strong, but it would have to do.

Five years after Jana's passing, our friend Daniel was

diagnosed with ALS. He asked Mary, me, and a couple of other close friends to help him on his final journey. During his last year, each time we sadly watched him lose the ability to bicycle, hike, and climb, I glimpsed the truth: If death could steal Daniel's joys, couldn't it steal mine? That took a wrecking ball to the wall. With squeals and groans, chunks tumbled down, littered my inner landscape. When the dust settled, there were still scattered remnants to hide behind. But everywhere else, the truth of aging, declining, and dying shattered my illusion and scared me. I mixed up more denial and started patching.

Three years after Daniel's death, Misty, one of the first people to befriend us when we moved to Oregon many years ago, was diagnosed with cancer for the second time and told this was a battle she couldn't win. An experienced hospice worker, she took the time to prepare her memorial service, start to finish. After Mary and I attended that touching service, I sensed that preparing my memorial service might ease my fears—if I stopped denying and started planning. A big if.

The same year Misty died, my brother, sister, and I moved our mother into a Delaware nursing home. As she has descended into the abyss of Alzheimer's, I have watched her memories depart, her personhood pass away. This leaves me frightened that I will follow her forgetful footsteps.

The deaths of Jana, Daniel, and Misty pounded the point home: I will die. Each cross-country visit to

Mom—three or four times a year—left me feeling that I was watching a painful preview of how death might take me. Scared and vulnerable, I took shelter behind the wall, clung to the illusion, acted as if nothing had changed. Until the summer that began with the exhausting North Cascades bike tour and the draining climb of South Sister.

That summer ended with a three-week adventure that started with a backpack trip deep into Wyoming's Wind River Range to climb that higher peak that we hoped South Sister had prepared us for. But hikers and stock trains, horses carrying riders and mules carrying cargo, crowded the trail we had to take to reach the base of the mountain. We managed to ignore the sight, sound, and smell of the multitude of trail users until we rounded a corner and came upon a dead pinto packhorse, swollen, stinking, and stiff-legged, beside the trail.

Hand over her nose, Mary said, "What in the world is that doing there?"

I shook my head in disbelief and said, "You got me."

"Are they just going to leave it there?"

"Well, I've heard that they sometimes remove dead stock in a sling under a helicopter. Or if that doesn't work, they blow it up."

"Blow it up? That's unbelievable," Mary said with disgust. "Let's get off this trail and find something resembling wilderness."

With the pain of climbing South Sister fresh in my

mind, I readily agreed to leave the trail and forgo the higher peak. We bushwhacked off trail and found an isolated spot barely big enough for our tent but overlooking a real gem of a lake.

We made ourselves a home and for each of the next three days we strolled the short distance from the campsite to the lake. There we played in the water, sunned ourselves on hot rocks, watched wildlife, and listened to the wind. I actually enjoyed *not* challenging myself. I loved *sitting still*! What was wrong with me?

After a few restful days, we packed out and drove north to Yellowstone and the next adventure. Several days into the backcountry, I sat in soothing shade alongside murmuring Coyote Creek, its streambed decorated with red and gold pebbles, tumbled smooth. I confessed to my journal that I feared the worst fate I could then imagine: turning into an old man who hears about others challenging themselves and mutters, "I used to do that."

At the end of our hike, Mary and I checked into a motel and stayed for the first time in Gardiner, Montana, at Yellowstone's north gate. After a good night's sleep, we took the steps from the motel down to a wooden deck thirty feet above the Yellowstone River. Off to our right, faint early-morning light kissed Electric Peak and turned the sky a purplish blue. The white noise of the river drowned all sound of the town's awakening. Mary, her face red from windburn, sat on a step adjusting our camp stove, adding the aroma of coffee to sage-scented air as the last day of our summer adventure began.

As I admired the high-desert landscape, the light swelled, transforming the river from black to dark green to aqua decorated with white caps and lighter green tongues and chutes. High clouds above Electric Peak glowed tangerine.

Watching the light change, I thought about how I had changed over the summer. Physically, my endurance for rigorous adventures had faded. Mentally, my confidence had wavered. Emotionally, frustration and fears now abounded.

I didn't share these scary revelations with Mary. I wasn't ready to accept them myself. What I didn't know then was how much more I had yet to face and accept in the wilds of aging.

CHAPTER 4

Heart Versus Mind

As that summer ended back home in Corvallis, Oregon, I felt so tired, so vulnerable, so afraid that I wondered if my body was failing me. Though I was not ill, had no malady, I began to obsess about death.

As fall clouds filled the sky, I admitted to Mary, Jim, and others that I might be finished with adventuring. Everyone found that hard to believe, probably because I didn't share the depth of my concerns. I wasn't willing to do that yet. Besides, I wanted to agree with Mary and my friends. But when I occasionally stopped denying, the admission that I might be finished adventuring felt painfully true.

As winter stormed in, Mary's mom—Mammaw to her kids, grandkids, and great-grandkids—started downhill, a slide toward the end that the family had been dreading for some time. But Mammaw pulled out of the slide, recovered under the loving care of Lois, the daughter she lived with. Then, a few weeks later, another dive, another recuperation. Lois called us every day with updates. Mary and I cringed each time the phone rang.

———

A couple of months before Mammaw's first slide, I had visited her in Baltimore. She had just turned eighty-nine and weighed less than eighty pounds. Every time I had seen her in the last couple of years, she had shrunk a bit more. But her mind stayed sharp. Mary and I kidded each other that her mom was the Incredible Shrinking Woman. And my mom was just the opposite: physically healthy with her mind disappearing. If we could magically combine those two, we would have one complete mother between us.

Though Mammaw was shrinking, her excitement was growing about reuniting with George, her husband who had passed away more than thirty years earlier. I talked with Mammaw about this when I had time alone with her during that visit.

She sat on a brown sofa, wrapped in a thick blue robe, pillows piled on either side to keep her erect. I sat in a chair across from her. Sunlight flooded the picture window behind her and created a glow around her head. On her left hand she still wore a gold band after decades as a widow.

"How do you picture the reunion with George?" I asked.

Mammaw, a devout Catholic, said, "I don't know

what form he'll have. I'm not even sure what form I'll have. But I'll know him." Her skeletal face glowed as she nodded. "I will."

I didn't tell Mammaw how much I envied her assurance, how I craved a clear picture of what will happen when I die.

But I did think about a similar conversation I had had with Daniel as ALS closed in on him. He had said that he believed in "light switch on/light switch off." He was certain that his body would simply go back to the earth: no heaven, no hell, no afterlife. Though that seemed an empty ending, my logical mind resonated with the idea. Yet my heart felt sad; if that's what happens when I die, I would never see Mary—or anyone else—again.

Mammaw, on the other hand, didn't see death as an ending; she pictured a happy reunion, an exciting beginning.

Wondering how that belief made her feel, I took a deep breath and asked, "Are you afraid of dying?"

She touched her thin white hair, then her hand drifted to rub the Bible on the end table. Finally, she said, "Aw, Honey, I'm not afraid. I know I'm going to heaven and meet God after all these years of waiting and praying." She stared at me, eyes sparkling. "What's there to fear?"

Indeed. If all that came to pass, what was there to fear? But I felt torn between heart and mind, between her heartfelt certainty of an afterlife and Daniel's logical certainty of the light switch turning off. That was my conflict, though, not Mammaw's. She knew what would happen when she died, and I didn't want to seem as if I doubted her.

"I'm so happy for you," I said. "But I hate to see you go."

She held my hand with her frail fingers, smiled, and said warmly, "I've had a great life, Honey. I'm ready."

I kissed her sunken cheek, knowing that was likely the last goodbye.

———

Since that talk, Mammaw's excitement about reuniting with George has prompted me to think *beyond* death. I see how Mammaw's welcoming death and believing in a joyful afterlife freed her from a fear of dying. Yet, I neither welcome death nor have any firm beliefs about afterlife. Perhaps that is something I need to change. But how?

CHAPTER 5

Meet Your Bear

AFTER THAT WORRISOME WINTER PASSED AND SPRING blossomed, the time came to arrange upcoming summer adventures. I faced a dilemma: I loved adventuring but sensed that if I was to grow through this floundering phase, I had to bail out of all upcoming external adventures with Mary and my friends and start a solo internal journey. I had to explore my fears, my mortality, and the concept of afterlife—the wilds of aging—just as I have explored wild lands.

Mary and my friends would eventually call this my morose period. Some saw it as an exercise in self-pity. But whether they liked it or not, whether I liked it or not, I felt compelled to make this my next adventure. Or, as Mary and I termed it on a trip to Yellowstone a few years ago, I had to meet my bear.

After we had spent several days and nights deep in

Yellowstone's backcountry and had grown more comfortable with its wildness, we planned to spend the day hiking into the middle of the upper Lamar Valley, where wolves, bison, and bears roam. We hoped to see some of these creatures, and the wide-open spaces of the valley would allow us to do so from a safe distance. We parked the car along the road, put on our daypacks, and started hiking toward the distant Lamar River.

As we walked along the valley floor, a solo hiker with long strides overtook us and stopped to chat. He looked to be about twenty-five years old. A faded green baseball cap pushed raggedly cut brown hair over the tops of his ears. His face was ruddy, with a strong chin accented by the red bandana around his neck.

When Mary asked where he was going, he turned away from us, pointed toward the distant mountains, and said that he had eleven more miles to go before reaching his campsite along the Lamar River.

While his back was turned to us, I studied his blue backpack. It was loaded, compact, and organized, the pack of an experienced hiker. That relieved me, as he was heading for a wild part of Yellowstone.

"Have you seen any wildlife?" Mary asked.

He turned back to us, smiled, and said, "I saw the same grizzly four times when I was camped along the Lamar last week."

"Four times?" I asked in amazement. "And you stayed?"

"Yeah. And it definitely knew I was there. One time

when I poked my head out of the tent it was upriver looking in my direction."

"That must have been a little scary," Mary said.

"It was," he said, tugging his cap down tighter onto his head. "And that's why I'm going back to the same spot."

"So you can see the griz again?" I asked.

"I sure hope so," he said with a dimpled smile.

After the hiker left, Mary and I walked on, holding hands and talking about him. He seemed like a capable backpacker, not a tourist in a hulking rented motor home asking where he might find a roadside bear to photograph. But still, he was returning to a potentially dangerous situation, one that had scared him just days earlier. He was, we decided, going to meet his bear.

That saying became shorthand we would use to describe intentionally going to places—mental, physical, or emotional—that scare us.

As I considered a solo journey to meet my bear, I understood that its challenges would not be measured in miles cycled or mountains climbed. Instead, the milestones would be emotions felt, bodily changes acknowledged, friends and loved ones lost, and maybe even wisdom gained.

Of course, I would journal, just as I had on adventures beside countless mountain streams or country roads. But on this journey I would write in our backyard.

And I would do more than write. After thirteen years away from serious gardening—at one time, digging in the garden was as predictable as spring equinox—I yearned to dig again, to see what I could nurture in the garden as I coaxed changes within myself. I would even try gardening year round, a new approach that would allow me to work—and write—in the garden whenever I needed to, be it spring, summer, fall, or winter. The garden would become my refuge where I could dig deeply into growing and dying.

As seasons came and went, I would see which plants grew, which feelings sprouted, which ideas blossomed. I would cultivate an understanding of where I had come from and where I was going now that the deaths of Jana, Daniel, and Misty and that tough summer of biking and hiking had finally smashed my wall, shattered that illusion of unending youth.

As my life felt up for grabs, I decided to meet my bear. To retreat to the garden.

CHAPTER 6

The Retreat

BUT FIRST I NEED A GARDEN TO RETREAT TO. OUR backyard, an intimate part of our small city lot, is enclosed on three sides by tall arborvitae, a ten-foot high wall of English ivy, and the back wall of our split-level house. Near that back wall is a tiny lettuce garden that has fit our schedule of adventuring and being away during each summer. That garden is bountiful in spring and fall and barren in summer.

But for my solo internal journey I want a different space. I want a space large enough to plant a fall garden while harvesting summer's, or to plant a winter garden while harvesting fall's. I want to create a space large enough to feel like a retreat.

I place a wheelbarrow beside the mound of steaming compost that was delivered to our driveway. I rhythmically shovel the wheelbarrow full, push it along the side of the house to the backyard, and dump it onto one of the four new garden beds I have decided to create. I inhale the compost's earthy aroma, return to the pile, and repeat. As I muscle into the work, sweat coats my forehead and runs down my back. Time enlarging the garden passes quickly in a soothing, meditative routine, broken occasionally by wondering how Mary is doing, tending Mammaw in Baltimore.

Last winter, as Mammaw slid and recovered, slid and recovered, Mary struggled with when to fly back to visit her mother.

"Should I go or should I wait?" Mary asked me as we sat at the dining room table after one of the many phone calls from Lois.

"I don't want to make two trips to the East Coast," I said. "And I had a great connection with Mammaw on our last visit. I feel complete with her, and I definitely want to be there with the family for the funeral. So I'm going to wait."

"Yeah, that makes sense," Mary said. But her frown told me that waiting—while worrying about another slide—might not work for her.

A few anxious weeks later we agreed on a plan. I would stay home and Mary would fly to Baltimore. If Mammaw was still living at the end of a week's stay, Mary would fly back. If her mom passed, Mary would have had the honor of helping her begin the journey to George. Relieved, Mary made plane reservations.

On the evening before Mary's flight, we walked

hand in hand through our backyard. We talked about my enlarging the garden while she was away, creating a space to plant and harvest, think and write.

———

And that's what I'm doing today: shoveling and sweating and hauling compost from the driveway to the new beds. When the March sun heats the garden and the sweat becomes unbearable, I take a break. Entering the French doors of our house, I tiptoe, trying to avoid tracking spring's abundant mud onto beige carpet. I notice I have a phone message. My heart beats faster as I wonder if this is Mary calling with *the* news. I listen to the message.

Mary speaks from three thousand miles away. "She's gone, Rick. Mom passed at twelve-ten eastern time today." She bursts into tears.

I slump onto the arm of the sofa and release a long, sad sigh.

Mary stops crying, sniffles, and speaks again. "She was surrounded by her family in a room filled with love and light. It was beautiful." Another pause, more tears. "I'll try to reach you later, but it's time for you to fly back."

The message ends but I remain seated, sweat cooling and stomach churning, remembering the last time I saw Mary's mom. When I rise and walk toward the French doors, I pay no attention to muddying the rug. Stepping outside, I stop, study the sky, the heavens where Mammaw was sure she would reconnect with George. I whisper, "Goodbye, Mammaw."

I walk to the garden, collect the shovel, rake, and wheelbarrow and put them away. I head into the house to book a red-eye to the funeral.

CHAPTER 7

Mammaw's Garden

AT THE FUNERAL MASS, MARY AND I SQUEEZED INTO THE crowded front pew of the large Catholic church Mammaw had attended almost every day until she was too weak to travel. All five of the church's priests—a testament to their respect for her—sat on the raised altar below a large crucifix. In front of the altar rested Mammaw's casket.

When communion began, two long rows of takers quickly filled the center aisle. I was one of the few who did not participate. I felt uncomfortable and guilty for not partaking, but my almost nonexistent religious training—my mom had dragged my brother, sister, and me to an Episcopal church for a few Christmas or Easter services—did not include anything close to communion.

Sitting in the empty pew, smelling incense and candle wax, I thought Mammaw would be happy to see so many family members and friends sharing this sacrament. A middle-aged woman with rapt expression approached the priest, partook of wine and wafer, and shuffled back to her seat.

What did she feel while taking communion? Did she feel something similar to what I once felt in the wild Beartooth Mountains, just north of Yellowstone?

———

Mary and I had hiked past a chain of alpine lakes to Becker Lake at 9,700 feet. The sky was cloudless. The fall sun was full but not warm. Reaching the lake, I stood on a sloping granite slab just where it disappeared into clear water.

I removed my windbreaker. Doffed down-filled vest. Shed shirt and t-shirt.

As wind whispered then roared, the temperature fell. I perched on the sun-warmed rock. Off came hiking boots and socks, pants and underwear.

I stood and faced the wind. Goose bumps rose. Though shivering, I felt exhilarated.

I knelt and dipped a red bandana into pure, cold lake water. I wrung the bandana and rubbed it gently over my upper body. This only pushed days of dirt around. But I was not trying for clean. I craved communion, to be one with this lake, a parishioner of the wild.

———

After flying from Mammaw's funeral back to Oregon, Mary and I dumped our luggage in the foyer of our house, bolted the front door, clung to each other, and vowed to cloister ourselves for the upcoming weekend. We needed to purge the stress of the death watch and funeral. We hoped the simple labor of working together to finish the four garden beds I had started would do that.

Side by side, we picked up where I had left off, hauling compost to the beds and then surrounding each with an accent of large and rounded red, green, beige, and mauve river rocks. By the end of the weekend, the beds were finished, our stress was diminished, and we were happy with the garden.

However, a couple of days later we were shocked when the first visitor to see the garden commented that the four beds looked like freshly covered graves. Oddly enough, Mary and I had not noticed this, but as soon as she heard the description, she wanted to reshape the beds. I disagreed.

Without consciously knowing it, I had designed the garden with four beds that represent the graves of loved ones lost: Jana, Daniel, Misty, and Mammaw. Each of their deaths had brought me closer to sitting in the garden. These four should be symbolically here, reminding me that death is always near, regardless of how I think or feel about it as my journey into the wilds of aging unfolds.

Mammaw's symbolic grave will help me recall her belief in a joyous reunion with George and God. It will help me remember to think beyond death, beyond the grave.

In her honor, we dubbed these four beds Mammaw's Garden.

CHAPTER 8

Jana

THE LAST TIME I SAW JANA, SHE WAS LYING IN BED, ARMS and face exposed, the rest of her wasted body barely evident beneath earth-toned blankets. The tight, natural auburn curls she had worn so proudly hung faded and limp.

"Do you want to raise my arms and give me some exercise?" she whispered to me.

How like her to want to feel her body move, to enjoy her kinetic spirit even as she lay dying.

"I'd love to," I said, grasping her bony fingers and sliding my other hand along her forearm, caressing its thinness.

"Oh, that feels good," she said, smiling. Her blue eyes—still so alive—locked onto mine until she closed them, and a tear slid down her jaundiced face.

I gently massaged her arm and said, "I love you, Jana."

"You're dripping," she replied with something like a giggle.

I wiped a tear from my cheek. "I've been doing that a lot lately."

I had never seen anyone fight for life, never witnessed such tremendous inner strength. I had the honor of watching Jana battle cancer with every weapon she could muster: conventional medicine, nontraditional medicine, spirituality, and sheer guts. At times I thought she was in denial. But I eventually realized I was wrong. She wasn't denying the likelihood of death, just as she wasn't denying the possibility she could live longer.

"I'm ready to go," Jana whispered. "It started yesterday. I couldn't get up. Can't raise my arms. I want to be free of this pain."

"Mary told me you envied your sister when she died last week."

"Yeah, she's free now," Jana said, closing her eyes. "She's said adios to her cancer pain."

I switched arms, felt no resistance, as if the arm no longer connected to her body. Recalling strength she once exuded, I said, "I remember how you used to ride that old three-speed bike to work, standing up, pedaling into a headwind, the whole ten miles. What an animal!"

"Yeah," she said, "and I remember the day I kicked your ass riding at Silver Falls State Park." She grinned until the right side of her face quivered through a spasm and her eyes closed.

I remembered that day too. She had humbled me, riding that same old three-speed, while I rode a lighter bike with at least twelve more gears. Yet, time and again, she had beaten me up tough hills with energy to spare.

I leaned over the bed to kiss her forehead, but she puckered so I kissed her lips lightly. They barely felt warm. "I want to see you again, Jana."

"You will," she whispered and closed her eyes.

I stood there, silent. I sensed she was leaving, and I wondered what she meant by saying I would see her again. Was she simply being her optimistic self, stating that she wasn't going to die yet and there would be time for another visit? That I could understand; that's what I had meant. Or was she saying that I would see her after she died? That was unexplored territory for me.

I heard the back door click open and thump closed. Mary and Jana's husband, Roger, slipped into the room. Roger and I hugged. He asked Jana if she wanted some quiet. She nodded. I stepped back and stood beside Mary, who slid her arm around me and pulled me close. We watched Roger hold a water bottle to Jana's lips, watched love flow between them.

When Jana finished drinking and closed her eyes, Roger moved beside us. Mary took his hand, and we walked outside and onto the porch of the house he had built. This was to have been their retirement nest where they would entertain friends, eat Roger's homemade bread, and spend quiet evenings in the hot tub counting stars. From here they would take winter jaunts to warm, sunny islands.

"It wasn't supposed to be like this," Mary said and hugged Roger, her arms unable to encircle his muscular chest and broad back.

As she sobbed, Roger's composure, strong in Jana's presence, crumbled. "It's like a bad movie," he said, bottom lip quivering. "I've got to watch it to the end. I don't want to, but there's nothing I can do." With a thick hand, calloused from years as an electrician, he covered his eyes and bent his head forward, chin on chest. "I hate seeing her in pain."

"You've done all you can, Roger," I said. "You can't fix this." I began to cry. "That's got to be so hard."

Roger looked off toward a distant Douglas fir–covered hill and shook his head side to side. "I saw it in her eyes the day I told her about her sister. I saw it! She gave up then. I was afraid she would. I even held off on telling her because of it. Damn it!" He ran a hand through his thick brown hair. More tears. "They weren't really all that close," he said with sad softness.

"But they were twins," Mary said.

Though Jana couldn't beat the scourge ravaging her athletic body, she could decide where and how—and maybe when—to exit. She did so with courage and grace. I can't imagine the pain she endured, don't want to imagine it. Yet she smiled, laughed, and loved right to the end, at age forty-three, eight years younger than I was. That she could die while so young and strong put that first crack—and a good-sized one—in my wall of denial.

But she also kick-started my wondering about what happens when a person dies. Like so many other aspects of death, I had avoided giving that question any thought. I might have stayed blissfully in denial—if Jana hadn't told me so confidently that I would see her again.

CHAPTER 9

The Raven

SEVERAL HOURS AFTER LEAVING JANA, ROGER, AND MARY,
I decided to ride my mountain bike up the gravel logging
road that switchbacks to the top of Dimple Hill and a
view of the valley in which we live. I had cycled up this
hill often, and I hoped the long climb would help me
work through the jumble of feelings about watching—
for the first time—a friend dying.

At the base of the hill, I clicked into the lowest gear
and found a rhythm for the steep climb. By the time
I reached a viewpoint a quarter mile below the peak
and stopped to look down into a ravine cut by a creek
and crowded with fir and bigleaf maple trees, I was
sweating, refreshed by endorphins, and ready to write.
I leaned the bike against a tree, pulled out my journal,
and sat on a moss-covered log. Words and tears flowed.

Pages later, I began to feel chilled. Looking up, I saw
a curtain of gray dangling from approaching clouds. I
stood and put vest and helmet on. I looked at the road.

Should I go down or continue climbing? The peak called. I mounted the bike and pedaled to the top and a view south. Though I couldn't see Roger and Jana's homestead, I knew it was out there in the thick of the storm now rushing toward me.

The wind began to bluster, and I realized I needed shelter. Behind me stood an imposing old-growth Douglas fir, its trunk as broad as the lichen-covered log bench it sheltered. Sighing wearily, I settled onto the bench and put on the last of my extra clothes. Spring in Oregon!

I huddled beneath the umbrella of the fir's huge lower limbs and watched the entire valley disappear under a gray pall of clouds and rain. I heard a strong wind making its way to the bench. When it hit, the old fir creaked and swayed. Small branches showered the ground, joining countless others from previous storms. I felt as if I was in a graveyard.

The gray curtain reached the hill and engulfed me. Hail rattled off my helmet, a sharp sound that blended with the deeper drone of hail ravaging the fir. The roar of an even stronger gust blasting the old tree obliterated all other sound. I put my head down and watched pea-sized hail bounce off my rain pants. My mind said go; my heart said stay.

When the downpour ended, I leaned back against the bench and looked toward Jana's house, where the sky was now clear. I saw a large bird soaring toward me, a raven, wings outstretched, traveling effortlessly on the wind. The bird passed right by the old fir—so close above me I heard its wings flapping. Ravens are not common in the valley we live in, and I felt a strong connection to the bird. At the same moment I wondered: Had Jana died? Was that her spirit departing?

Watching the raven go, I felt compelled to whisper, "Goodbye, Jana."

Moments later, the clouds broke apart and sun lit the valley. Weather beaten, emotionally drained, and wondering what had just happened, I climbed on my bike and cycled down the road, sometimes pedaling hard, eager to reach the sanctuary of home, sometimes riding the brakes, reluctant to leave this sanctuary of spirit.

A few hours later, Mary called me at home and said that Jana had died that afternoon. My face flushed, my stomach tightened, and tears formed, but all I said was, "Oh, no."

"Sometime after you and I left," Mary said, "Jana slipped into unconsciousness. Then her heart and breathing stopped. Paramedics arrived, and somehow she came back to life. She asked them how long she had been gone, and they said about thirty minutes. Then Jana said, 'Thirty minutes? That means nothing to me.'"

We chuckled with love at the image of Jana continuing to battle death right to the finish line. So Jana.

I remembered the storm and the raven and asked, "What time did she die?"

"It was around three."

"Oh, God," I said with a rush of tears, "that's when I saw the bird."

Had I seen Jana again, just like she had promised?

In retrospect, I understand that my heart took me to the top of Dimple Hill all those years ago. My heart kept me there through a ferocious storm until I saw that raven riding a strong wind, heading north. I somehow sensed I might be seeing Jana's unbeatable spirit depart. The phone call from Mary confirmed the timing was right, added logical support to my sensing. But something brought me to tears that day.

Tears aren't logic; they're my heart's way of opening me to seeing new things. If I could see Jana's spirit flying north, what else could I see? What else was I missing? Could I see her in an afterlife? Is that what she had meant earlier that day when she promised I would see her again? Were the tears my heart's way of pointing me to those unsettling questions I had not considered until that stormy moment years ago?

But now my mind challenges: How could that raven have been Jana or her spirit? Wasn't the bird simply a powerful metaphor?

My mind wants a logical explanation. My heart doesn't need one.

CHAPTER 10

Voices Inside

I HAVE CONTINUED TO ENLARGE MY GARDEN RETREAT. A couple of weeks ago I spent hours on hands and knees yanking English ivy from a spot it had usurped and I aimed to reclaim. Now, as I chip away at the rock-infested clay where the ivy was, I repeatedly bang rocks with the shovel blade. Each hit fires a bolt of pain up my already aching left arm—a result of the bout with the ivy.

One especially painful hit activates within me the cutting voice of my long-dead father: *You ain't never gonna get this right. Why don't you just quit?* I stop digging and stand tall, shifting the shovel handle from one hand to the other, waiting for the pain to subside, trying—and failing—to ignore him. Throughout my adult life his cruel comments have questioned my ability and challenged my confidence, just as they are doing today.

I study the bank I need to cut into. The cut is deep. Deeper than I had figured. Maybe too deep for my ailing arm. I need a space about six feet long and a foot and a half wide. Though this is about the size of a narrow grave—my retreat seems to generate death-related images—the space is actually for a planter box with an attached trellis that I spent the previous week building. The cedar and bamboo structure turned out better than expected despite zingers from Dad. The trellis will work perfectly to block the view of the garden's growing compost pile. It will also double as the home for an ornamental grape and some colorful climbing nasturtiums that will brighten this corner.

The space for the planter would be no problem just about anywhere else on our mostly flat city lot. Now that I think about it, I'm digging into the only incline left on the property. *Why didn't you think of that before you started this job?* Dead Old Dad's snide voice nags. I cringe.

Mary, pushing a wheelbarrow past Mammaw's Garden, stops beside me, sets it down, and takes her time surveying my lack of progress. "That's a lot of dirt to dig," she says. "Is your arm up to it? You told me it bothered you after clearing the ivy."

I bend my left arm several times, feel shooting pain, and worry this injury is another sign of my body declining with age. But I refuse to wince. Instead, I force a smile and lie, "I don't think it'll be a problem."

Mary stares at me in frank disbelief and says, "I just don't want you to hurt yourself." She hoists the wheelbarrow and pushes on toward the front yard. "Take it easy," she yells over her shoulder.

I smile at her caring and turn back to the task. I wonder how to dig a big enough flat spot in the bank without doing more damage to my elbow. And my confidence.

I return to digging. The rocks haven't left. The clang of metal on rock, the sight of sparks flying off the blade, and my growing doubt that I can do what this job requires drag me back to a painful day decades ago with my father.

———

I had just graduated high school and was working beside Dad. For three days I had been digging a ditch, removing hard-packed clay, rocks, and oak tree roots. The ditch would hold the foundation of an extension to the large home of our boss, a rich, successful man my father worked for and worshipped. Dad laid out the project and would pour the concrete foundation. I got to battle the ditch with pick and shovel. He told me that if I did well, there might be a better job for me elsewhere in the boss's small empire. I could follow in Dad's footsteps.

When the pick smashed into a rock, a shock wave blasted through my hands, up my arms, and into my head. By ten o'clock, I hurt all over. During our break, I wondered whether this was all there would be to life after high school: a pick, a shovel, and a never-ending ditch. I sighed loudly, drawing a glare from Dad as he sipped hot black coffee and smoked a cigarette. A few moments later, without a word, he stood, brushed dirt off his khaki pants, flicked the still smoking cigarette into the ditch, and motioned me to get up and get back to work.

Two hours later, at lunch, I collapsed in the shade with my back against an oak tree. Trying to recharge, I chugged a chocolate drink and wolfed a peanut butter and jelly sandwich. By the end of the half hour, I was stiff and craving a nap. As my eyes slid shut and I drifted into an adolescent dream starring my girlfriend, Dad brought me back to reality by booming in a marching cadence a drill sergeant's song he had learned during paratrooper training in World War II: "Off your ass and on your feet. This is reveille, not retreat."

I cursed under my breath, grabbed pick and shovel, and stepped back into the ditch and the full sun. As I fought rocks and roots, sweat flooded my eyes. The pick slipped through my sweaty hands. Blisters popped; salty sweat added insult to injury. I obsessed on thoughts as intense as the struggle with the ditch: *I can't go on like this. I hate this work. I don't want to break my body on this rich man's house. I don't care if he ever gets this extension built. I want to quit!*

But what would Dad say?

I peeked at him, hoping he hadn't noticed that some of the water trickling down my cheeks was tears. I wiped my face with a dirty hand and kept digging.

By two o'clock I was fighting with a rock three times the size of the shovel blade. I couldn't go around it or through it. I had to deal with that rock just like I had to deal with my fierce desire to quit. I whacked the rock with the pick; sparks flew. Hoping I might dislodge the rock, I pried with the shovel; the hickory handle bent. Crack! The handle snapped. I fell backward and landed with a thud in a pile of red clay. I lay there smelling my sweat, tasting defeat.

I snapped. "That's it, Dad! I can't take this anymore. I QUIT!"

Dad looked up from his measuring tape, slid a pencil behind his ear. No pick and shovel for him. He stared at me, then glanced at the ditch, the oak tree, and back to me. "You gonna let this job get the best of you, Boy? You just gonna give up?" He brushed flecks of dirt off his clean, white t-shirt. "What the hell kinda kid have I raised?"

I couldn't answer. Flat on my back, crying and ashamed, I couldn't speak at all.

Dad shook his head side to side. "So you're quittin'?"

You're damn right, I thought, as I nodded without a word.

The crinkling of cellophane as he dug a cigarette from a pack broke the silence. A match hissed. Smoke rose toward the bright sun. I looked at my father's face through the blue haze. He stared down at me as if he didn't know me.

He snuck a glance at the boss's house, surely wondering if his idol was watching me fail. And if I failed, what would that say about Dad as a father, as a man?

He turned back to me, ran his hand through his red hair, and quietly, menacingly, said, "Go on. Quit. But you better have another job by the time I get home."

He grabbed the pick, turned his back on me, walked away, and yelled over his shoulder, "Get outa here, Boy. I got work to do."

I rubbed away tears with clay-stained hands, got to my feet, and slipped away from Dad and the ditch.

CHAPTER 11

Ben-isms

I KNOW NOW THAT SOMETHING CHANGED FOREVER WHILE I battled those rocks under that old oak. As Dad used to say, especially after a few too many beers, "Don't end up like me, Boy. Make somethin' of yourself." That hot, painful day was my start of doing just that.

After quitting and leaving that ditch to Dad, I rushed home, cleaned myself up, and went to a nearby warehouse that I had heard was always hiring. I had a job there by the time Dad came home. As time passed, I went from that warehouse to enlisting in the army, to installing telephones, to completing college, to remodeling homes, to crafting stained glass, to waiting tables, to managing a restaurant. Sometimes I wondered if I would ever settle into one career.

Finally, I followed one piece of Dad's cutting advice: *Make sure you get a job usin' your head, Boy. You'll starve if you have to do somethin' with your hands.* With my decade-old bachelor's degree in psychology, I settled into a career as a vocational rehabilitation counselor. My catalog of jobs, I would soon discover, had been my apprenticeship, had helped me understand the world of work and succeed as a rehab counselor.

I spent the next twenty-six years working with clients, most of them men, middle-aged or older. Each had been disabled by an on-the-job injury. Many were tough guys from hard jobs: construction workers and cops, loggers and fishermen, truck drivers and freight handlers. I helped them discover that there was life after injury. I assisted each in choosing a new career that his damaged body could handle. I supported them as they overcame confusion, fear, loss, and disability and moved ahead into school or on-the-job training. Once they completed training, I helped them find a job that used their new skills.

The toughest clients for me were those who looked, acted, or even sounded like my father. With them I sometimes felt like an unsure kid instead of a seasoned professional. I had to remind myself that the client was not my father, and I was no longer that kid.

I enjoyed my career and learned, contrary to what the boy had feared, there was much more to my work life than a pick, a shovel, and a never-ending ditch.

But now with just months to go until retiring from that career, I still haven't learned to silence my father's criticism, the cutting remarks I named after him, the Ben-isms. Though Ben is long gone, I dread he will hound me for as long as I live. But each time I prove him wrong—*that cedar and bamboo planter fit just fine, Dad*—feels like a small victory.

Still, the intensity of the last clash in my garden retreat surprises me, reminds me I'm always my father's son, and makes me wonder how that critical father who lurks inside me fits into my exploration of the wilds of aging. His death twenty-four years ago did not drive me to denial or damage my illusion of immortality. His death is not one of the reasons I retreated. Yet here he is, badgering and belittling: *"You ain't never gonna get this right. Why don't you just quit?"* That dig makes me question whether I have what it takes to finish. It also makes me expect he'll visit again whether I want him to or not.

With or without Dead Old Dad, reflecting and writing in this garden is how I will dig through the hard-packed clay, rocks, and roots of my vulnerability, questions, and fears. Dad's comments won't make the digging easier. Just as they didn't under that oak so long ago.

CHAPTER 12

Patience

THE LAST ENCOUNTER WITH DAD AND THE DREAD OF more battles make me wonder how long I'll be able to sit in this garden before I run out of patience. I know I'm in for a long ride. I've denied thinking about aging, physical decline, and mortality all my life; change won't come overnight. But patience is not my strong suit. How long will this journey into the wilds of aging take?

Today the garden mirrors my inner turmoil. As I slump on a wooden chair and glare, the overhang of the house roof protects me from incessant rain. All week an unusual—even for June—monsoon-like storm has dumped record-breaking rain on Oregon. The fretful tapping of raindrops drenching the magnolia accompanies the raucous calling of crows. The garden hangs in suspended animation, frustrating me and trying my patience. Rain, rain, rain!

I rise and stomp over to the short rows of carrots that Mary and I seeded with fanfare sixty-five days ago, one of the first plantings in Mammaw's Garden. According to the seed catalog, we should be crunching eight-inch Napas now and salivating over a harvest of ten-inch Purple Haze carrots by next week. Kneeling in the rain, I pull one plant from the Purple Haze row, one from the Napa row. Neither looks like a carrot. Both are as long as my little finger but white and twine thin.

I stand, toss the carrots onto the compost pile, and tell myself to be patient. The seeds were cultivated on a farm near here. Our raised beds, though new, are a nourishing, crumbly mix of compost and clay. The plants should grow. But having just returned to the garden after years of seeking external adventures, I lack recent gardening success to help me cultivate patience.

As I plod back to the chair, I mutter to the garden, "Grow, grow, grow!" Seated under the protection of the overhang, I realize that now is a good time to consider lessons about patience that I learned from adventures "out there" that might be useful "in here." I zip my jacket, settle back, close my eyes, and tune in to the subtle drone of traffic a couple of blocks away. Bit by bit the images of a hilly road, a bicycle, and a long day's ride materialize.

On the morning of the day I recall, Jim and I awoke at a campsite in Idaho. We were two-thirds of the way into our first long bicycle tour and would cycle a total of seven hundred miles as we followed the Lewis and Clark bike trail over three mountain ranges from Astoria, Oregon, to Missoula, Montana.

We had taken down our tents and were loading our bikes and trailers when I discovered a flat tire on my bike. I started the repair—a multi-step process that I hate. All went well until, impatient to finish and stop wasting valuable morning time, I yanked on the new tube's valve stem and broke it off.

"*Well, ain't you handy,*" Dead Old Dad sneered, "*you just turned one flat into two.*"

Yes, Dad was on the tour too.

By the time I finished, Jim and I had lost an hour and a half of riding time. With more than fifty miles to cycle, we hit the road. And what a road, every mile a time-sucking uphill, especially dragging fifty-pound trailers.

We were climbing Idaho Highway 95, a two-lane road busy with roaring trucks that sucked us into their slipstream. Our guidebook revealed that we had a few miles before we would arrive at an intersection with Old Winchester Road. Once there, we could choose one road or the other. When we reached that intersection, we pulled off to talk and refuel with a couple of bananas. We confessed to being impatient to get these hills, the remaining miles, and this day behind us.

So far Highway 95 had been a smooth road with good shoulders. But our guidebook was mum about hills that might lurk ahead. For comparison, I read aloud passages describing numerous steep climbs and descents on the alternate route, Old Winchester Road. When I finished, we watched a battered pickup cough foul-smelling black smoke and slowly climb Old Winchester.

"Oof, that looks steep," Jim said around a mouthful of banana.

I swallowed the last of mine and said, "I vote for 95."

"I can go with that too," Jim said.

As we pedaled on, the ride went from demanding to surreal. The road curved again and again. Rounding each curve, I hoped to see the hill's crest. When I didn't, frustration and impatience grew. Finally, I could stand no more. I beat on the handlebars and yelled at the top of my lungs, "Arrgh!"

From behind I heard Jim's muffled question: "Crest?"

I laughed as I realized he was as impatient as I was. I feared we would never reach a crest, that we had entered climbing purgatory. Grasping for anything to keep me going, I thought about other long climbs I have had the pleasure—and pain—of meeting on my bike. After I pictured myself cresting each climb, I looked around and yelled at Highway 95, "I can outlast you!" But I wasn't sure. This time Jim didn't hear me; he had pulled far ahead.

After another tiring mile, the grade started to ease, a sign, I hoped, that the crest, our campsite, and the day's end were near. I shifted up one gear from my lowest and started a sluggish sprint to the finish. To my right, I heard stones crash down the hillside. I jerked my head toward the sound and saw a mule deer, a six-point buck, running effortlessly up a rocky, steep slope toward the conifer forest. He stopped and stared at me, his nostrils flaring, proud eyes wide. I would have liked to stay and meet his gaze, perhaps photograph him, but impatience reigned. And the end of the day's torture was so close.

I turned away, put my head down, and pushed on, trying to catch Jim.

Now as I sit in the garden listening to the murmur of June's rain, I consider how climbing Highway 95 taught patience. There was no way to climb that hill any faster; I struggled to climb it at all. I had to believe I had prepared for the climb, and the hill could not go on forever. I had to slowly pedal on in my lowest gear, keep my head down, and avoid staring at the hill yet to come. Patient pedaling gained the top.

Studying our stunted garden, I translate that hard-earned cycling lesson into a gardening lesson. There's no way to make this garden grow faster; it's struggling to grow at all. I have to believe that I have prepared this plot well and the inclement weather will not last forever. I have to patiently keep weeding, fertilizing, and thinning. Eventually I'll find a succulent carrot to crunch.

And there's an even bigger lesson from out there for in here. There's no way to rush this journey into the wilds of aging. I must believe that sixty years of life have prepared me, and this long, slow struggle with questions and doubts will not last forever. I must patiently sit, reflect, write, and even deal with Dad. Eventually, I'll reach some conclusions that satisfy.

CHAPTER 13

Daniel

EIGHT YEARS BEFORE I RETREATED TO THE GARDEN, OUR friend Daniel retired from his geologist job. He was fifty-six and wanted to have the time and energy for things he truly wanted to do: writing articles about outdoor adventures, teaching classes on bicycle repair, and hiking and skiing with an eighty-pound backpack across 120 miles of Alaskan glaciers and ice fields.

It was good he didn't wait. Within three years of retiring he sent this e-mail to a small group of friends.

Two years ago I was privileged to be one of a group of four that crossed the Juneau Icefield. When the going got tough, one of us would shout out: "Remember, this is an expedition not a camping trip." This was a reminder that we were there voluntarily and that we had to rely on each other, and only on each other, to get to Juneau. It was a rallying cry. We wanted no outside help. We had elected to take no Sherpas along to carry the load. We pulled together and the team reached our goal.

Now I am starting on a new journey. Although I will reach the destination alone, I will need a huge amount of help along the way. I hope that I can count on your help as a Sherpa on my journey.

I have ALS. No treatment is known. Two to five years is a common range of life expectancy as nerves stop functioning and muscles atrophy.

I would prefer to tell each of you this news individually but I don't have enough courage or enough tears. I love all of you; let's make the most of the rest of the time that we get to share together.

The day Mary and I received that e-mail, we rushed to Daniel's side. With tears and hugs we talked with him about the shock and injustice of his deadly diagnosis. Without reservation, we agreed to be Sherpas and help Daniel and his wife, Joanne, on his final journey.

At first, Daniel, Mary, and I could still bicycle together as we had so many other times. But soon we witnessed how ALS eats away at motor neurons, the little fibers that control muscles. Every day, every hour, every minute, Daniel lost some ability to fire muscles. With disuse, his muscles atrophied. And as they did, the bike rides got shorter and slower. And sweeter; we never knew if we would take another ride as a threesome.

When his balance deteriorated, we lent him our two-wheeled recumbent bike, hoping that the low, upright seating would help him ride for a few more weeks. One day Mary and I watched him push off with one weak leg and wobble down the street on the bike. Halfway through the block he coasted to a stop and placed his feet on the ground. When he tried to start, he couldn't get enough speed for stability. When he lifted both feet to the pedals, he fell over. I winced and felt like a dad watching his kid on a first bike ride. But I was watching my fifty-nine-year-old friend struggling to take one of his last.

Though two-wheeled bicycling proved impossible, Daniel wasn't ready to stop. Harry and Holly, Daniel's adult son and daughter, bought him a shiny new, cherry-red recumbent with three wheels. Stability was no longer an issue; he didn't fall over. But as muscles continued to deteriorate and he lost grip strength, he had trouble squeezing the bike's hand brakes.

Though Daniel couldn't stop, he still longed to go. Always a problem solver, he arranged to ride on a tandem behind his friend Jack around the Grand Loop in Yellowstone National Park. Daniel could pedal, didn't have to brake, and was out with someone he loved in wild lands he worshipped.

Other friends and family helped with activities he could no longer do alone. His wife, both kids, and a couple of friends went climbing with him in the mountains of Colorado. Mostly, Daniel was harnessed, hooked to ropes, and assisted during the whole climb. But he did it. And on one section, Harry swung over, put his arm around Daniel, and said, "I love you, Dad." Even before he lost so much physical ability, Daniel couldn't have climbed higher than his son's words and touch made him feel at that moment.

CHAPTER 14

Light Switch Off

A FEW MONTHS AFTER DANIEL RETURNED FROM MOUNTAIN climbing, he and I were seated on the back porch, watching birds hit the many feeders in his backyard.

After we made some small talk, I said to him, "I understand that you don't believe in life after death."

He thought for a moment, tears welled up, and he replied, "I don't see a need for it."

I took his hand and said softly, "I was really just thinking about myself. If there's life after death, maybe I'd get to see you again."

His lips smiled; his eyes frowned. "Sorry."

As the afternoon passed and the birds flitted here and there, we talked more about what would happen when he died. Daniel said that he was a scientist and held a scientific view: his body would stop functioning and start returning to the earth. He would cease to exist as a person. When I asked about his spirit, he said he did not believe that a person's spirit left their body and went elsewhere. There was nothing beyond the life lived every day. "Light switch on/light switch off" was how he saw dying. One minute you're here, the next you're not. Daniel would not expect me to see his spirit flying north on a strong wind.

A few days later, I went as usual with Daniel to his water therapy at the local aquatics center. I used a lift to lower him into the pool where a physical therapist helped him and some others in a series of exercises. When the session ended, I lifted him out of the pool and rolled him in his wheelchair to the locker room. There, as I washed his hair, he admitted that the end was near. I asked how that felt. Prompting like this previously had led to deep sharing between us.

But this time he simply said, "I've never been much for self-analysis."

I stopped asking questions.

Later that day as I replayed that conversation in my head, I realized that Daniel had turned another corner. He no longer needed to plumb the depths of death and dying. He was ready to go.

The following Thursday morning Mary and I went to his house and bathed, shaved, and dressed him. We used a mechanical lift to help him into his large tan recliner and covered him with a dark blue blanket. I read him a story about his impact on my life that I had written while on a recent multiday bike tour with Mary along the Oregon coast. Daniel, the geologist, laughed at my mistaken identification of a coastal landform. Daniel, the man, cried when I read of the grief I felt while watching ALS steal his joys: a strong cyclist now confined to a wheelchair, an adventurer now barely able to scratch his nose, a teacher no longer able to convey concepts, a writer unable to make his computer's speech-activated software understand his slurred words.

On Sunday night Mary and I phoned Joanne and asked if we should come by on Monday morning to bathe and dress Daniel. Joanne didn't think that would be necessary. The kids had returned home, and she had plenty of help on what she believed was the last leg of Daniel's journey.

To end his journey, Daniel had chosen to stop eating and drinking rather than swallow the pills prescribed for his use under Oregon's assisted suicide program. He would not have been able to grasp the pills and put them in his mouth; he would need help. A gentle, caring man, Daniel did not want to burden anyone with the memory of giving him the final pill. Instead, friends and family would fondly recall spraying a cooling mist of water into his mouth or treating him to an ice chip.

After the phone call to Joanne, Mary and I snuggled on our sofa, reminiscing about Daniel, ALS, and being Sherpas. Then we went to bed. This dream followed.

I was the pilot of "the president's" jet. I knew that I was not a real pilot, was surprised to learn that I could fly a plane at all. Nonetheless, I joined the president's small entourage exiting the plane, heading for a conference.

The conference room was tiny; there were few attendees. The president found a seat at a classroom-style desk, accepted a paper on a subject, and dove into reading. In short order, the conference ended and the president left the room, me and the entourage in tow.

As I stepped out of the conference room, I realized that I had forgotten my jacket. I went back into the room, found a pile of jackets, but couldn't find mine. I decided to "borrow" a blue nylon windbreaker. Although the borrowed jacket didn't fit me, it would have to do. I had to fly the president to his next destination.

I rushed from the room but couldn't find the president's group. Instead, I walked alone along the streets of a small town, searching everywhere for the airport. I worried that the president could not take off without me. Then I recalled that I didn't know how to fly a plane, didn't know the first thing about successful takeoff. Maybe the president was better off without me. He'd find someone else to take him to his next stop.

On Monday morning, over breakfast, I shared the dream with Mary. She took a sip of coffee, thought for a moment, and said, "I think it's about helping Daniel on his journey as far as you could go. Even though you didn't know how to fly the plane, how to be a Sherpa, you did your best and landed him safely. Now, as he approaches death, you can't join him on the next leg of the journey."

Her interpretation resonated. Daniel actually was a president—of the board of a local nonprofit land conservation organization—when I met him. And I clearly had no idea what I had signed up for when I agreed to be one of his Sherpas. Though I will always treasure my time helping Daniel on his final journey.

CHAPTER 15

Powerful Heart

SEVERAL HOURS AFTER I SHARED MY DREAM WITH MARY, she called from work to tell me that Daniel had died the previous night. With wife and kids by his side, he just stopped breathing.

After the phone call, I kept working, writing a report on an injured worker's progress toward finding a new career. I could easily have stopped, since I was working at home. Continuing to work struck me as odd, until I realized that I had been preparing for this moment for fourteen months.

Finally, I went upstairs and put on some music so I could sing a farewell to Daniel. But I didn't picture him as I sang loudly and soulfully. Instead, I imagined singing to mourners at his memorial service. Mulling over this discrepancy, I realized I had said everything I needed to say to Daniel, as he had to me. He had ended one journey, and I could not help him on the next, just as in the dream about Daniel as president.

Surely that dream was my heart speaking. While Daniel believed that his light switch had turned off, that there was nothing more, and while that belief made logical sense to my mind, my heart believed a different story. My heart—through the dream—was telling me that Daniel was continuing his journey, going elsewhere. But where?

Though I couldn't answer that question, the fact that he had a destination hinted at an afterlife. If I believed my heart, that is. But why listen to my heart instead of my mind?

A book, *The Heart Speaks,* takes on that question. The author, Mimi Guarneri, MD, points out that Western science teaches that the brain rules the communication network of our body. The brain responds to external stimuli and generates emotions. The heart, says Western science, is just a pump that keeps the body going.

But Guarneri, founder and medical director of Scripps Center for Integrative Medicine, cites research in the 1960s and 1970s by John and Beatrice Lacey that showed otherwise. "The heart, the Laceys discovered, was not just a pump but also an organ of great intelligence, with its own nervous system, decision making powers, and connections to the brain. They found that the heart actually 'talks' with the brain, communicating with it in ways that affect how we perceive and react to the world."

She also describes research by Dr. J. Andrew Armour, which found that the heart sends signals to the brain that affect our reasons, choices, emotions, and perceptions.

Guarneri's years of experience as a cardiologist have convinced her that the heart is more important for our survival than the brain. The heart is formed before the brain and stops after the brain dies. Life can continue without the brain, but not without the heart. Also, the heart's electromagnetic current and energy field are stronger than those of the brain. Finally, the heart is more sensitive, beating with different rhythms to different emotions.

She asks a question: "But what if it's not the brain telling the heart what to feel, but the heart informing the rest of the body? What if changing the mind actually involves changing the heart?" That question gives new meaning to the phrase *listen to your heart*, cuts right to the core of my mind-heart debate.

I reflect again on the contrast between Daniel's view and Mammaw's. My mind agrees with Daniel's logical notion of light switch on/light switch off: once my body dies, I'm done. But my heart beats with Mammaw's joyous belief: once she dies, she'll meet with George and God. Though I don't know if there's a God I'll ever meet, one who looks out for me, I still desire her inviting image of reconnecting with loved ones.

CHAPTER 16

Quiet Mind

Three months have passed since I began journaling in the garden. Summer solstice beckons. How fitting. Solstice is a combination of Latin words that mean "sun" and "still." And sitting still in the sun—now that Oregon's famous rain stopped a couple of weeks ago—is what I've been doing.

Journaling about the wilds of aging has been like visiting a "paper therapist." I rarely come to the garden with a specific topic in mind. Instead, I sit, look around, and free write, putting words to paper without editing, evaluating, or judging. Most days this works well. The writing, like roots seeking water, drills down from external description to internal discovery. Some days when I finish, I pump my fist into the air in celebration. Other days I sniffle and wipe away tears.

Today, as I sit in a lawn chair, pen in hand, journal in my lap, I'm like a dog turning in circles, sniffing for a spot to lie in. Distractions abound. The acrid smell of elderberry blooms assails my olfactory sense. The muted pounding of hammers from house construction a few blocks away gives the neighborhood a disturbing, erratic pulse.

Will I settle in?

This is so unlike the start of an external adventure, where at this time of the morning I'd be preparing for a kinetic day of hiking, biking, or canoeing. The promise of new sights, sounds, and smells would charge me with excitement. But sitting here in the garden, I'm where I'll be in an hour, or two, or four. Though that brings little excitement today, I remind myself that I chose to be here. I may as well try to be truly present.

A breeze plays the sets of chimes that hang from the large and thickly leafed magnolia tree, the centerpiece of our backyard. Bamboo chimes clunk endearingly while the soft, haunting harmonies of our tuned chimes drift through me.

I settle back, take some deep relaxing breaths, and let my eyes explore the garden. A flower bed sits just in front of me. This multilevel bed overflows with such an abundance of colors, shapes, sizes, and textures that Mary and I call it the Riot Garden. Some of the tall, bright green, backlit, sword blades of crocosmia contrast sharply with other blades wrapped in shadows. A tall fennel crowning the highest mound looks like a giant tree in a pastoral Japanese painting. On a lower mound, fuzzy heads of chives create a light purple constellation in the surrounding green galaxy.

The angry barking of a dog up the street jars me out of the moment. I sigh and continue to sit.

I close my eyes and zero in on the soft sounds that haunt the morning: the bubbling of our small backyard fountain, the rustle of the magnolia's leaves, the whisper of wind through fir needles, the twittering of tiny birds hiding in the arborvitae, the tapping of a scrub jay's claws as it dances across the metal patio table.

I turn my head and open my eyes. I gaze at Mammaw's Garden and a raised bed outlined by the colorful river rock we placed there. Patient weeding, fertilizing, and thinning have paid off. The bed is backed by light green pea vines that have climbed a trellis nearly to the rain gutters of our house. Inch-long edible pods hang below white blossoms. In front of the trellis the bed brims with darker greens of spinach, beets, and chard.

The sun warms me and I remove my hat and unzip my windbreaker. As my face, chest, thighs, and shins warm, I feel like a cat sitting in a sunny window. I fully recline the back of the lawn chair, drop pen and journal to the ground, and turn onto my stomach. My closed eye pressing against my forearm creates a field of red dots intermingled with golden threads in the darkness. A breeze carrying the sweet aroma of sun-warmed bark mulch again plays the chimes; the wind song makes me smile.

My mind empties. Time evaporates. Questions fade. Doubts disappear.

I hear my heart beat, feel each muscular contraction. I sense the blood coursing through my body, fueling my brain.

Maybe the heart does control everything. Because when I finally quiet my mind, heart is all that remains.

CHAPTER 17

Riding the Conflict

Solstice has slipped away. though the days are slightly shorter, the garden still basks in July's ample light and heat. There is little to do but watch plants grow. I have time for another visit to Mom.

Mom lives in a Delaware nursing home where she is deteriorating with Alzheimer's. My brother, sister, and I moved her there once providing home care became too difficult for my sister, who has always lived near Mom in Delaware.

Though I lived in Oregon, too far away to provide home care, Mom's descent through the stages of the disease has challenged me too.

Late in the first stage, my regular long-distance phone calls to Mom grew more difficult. When she failed to complete a sentence or lost track of an entire thought, she stopped talking, and I felt her frustration. Over time, she cut the phone calls shorter and shorter until I finally understood that I should just not call. I stopped. And felt guilty.

In the second stage, history slipped away. She forgot not only events in the present but also significant events and people in her past. She couldn't identify that man in her wedding picture—her first, only, and ex husband. She hasn't said my name in several years.

As Mom drifts toward the third and final stage, she requires close monitoring by nursing home staff. She can still feed herself—when she chooses to eat—but she's losing control of her bowels. She's weak and needs help to walk.

Each trip to visit Mom—I make three or four a year—brings up the same feelings. I long to be a good son and visit, but seeing her hurts. I hate the condition she's in. She doesn't know me, and I wonder if my visits bring her any joy at all. I'd stop in a heartbeat if I knew they didn't. But I feel guilty about not wanting to go. After all, she's the one trapped in her body in a nursing home. Believing that the visits bring her some joy is a leap of faith I'm willing to pay the emotional price for.

Riding this conflict, I fly to Baltimore, rent a car, and drive south toward Mom. Fifteen hours after leaving Oregon, I sit and sweat in the stuffy car in a hot parking lot, hesitant to go inside the nursing home. On the last two visits, I found Mom going downhill, weight dropping, energy flagging, eyes sinking. I fear worse now. I wipe my forehead, look over at the long, one-story building, and find her window. The venetian blinds, broken in two spots, are down, shutting out the sunny day. I step out of the car, take a deep breath of humid air, and plod to the entrance.

The front door opens easily, but after I enter I hear the creepy click of the door's automatic lock that keeps disoriented residents from escaping. I smell pine-scented disinfectant and pass an always-empty couch flanked by a freestanding photo display of smiling—and never aging—residents. As I turn a corner, my shoes squeak on linoleum.

I reach the brightly fluorescent-lit nursing station and watch as an older—but healthy looking—woman approaches the station and rattles off a series of non-sensical questions. A nurse seated at the station pulls a phone away from her ear, puts a hand over the receiver, and says to the woman, as if she's done this many times before, "Okay, Virginia, I'm busy right now. I'm on the phone. You'll just have to go sit down." The nurse points to a row of worn cushioned chairs lining a wall, many filled just after lunch with napping residents. One of them, a woman, rocks back and forth, keening softly. Virginia, firing questions to no one, shuffles toward the chairs.

The nurse turns to me, smiles with recognition, and points down a long hallway. "She's in her room."

CHAPTER 18

Mom's Nightmare

As I ENTER MOM'S ROOM, SHE LOOKS UP FROM THE COM-fortable stuffed chair that once sat in her living room and now crowds the only window in this small room. Her mouth hints at a smile, and I see she's not wearing her upper dentures. Her eyes reveal no recognition, so I proclaim in a sing-song voice, "Mommy, Mommy, Mommy! It's your son, Rick, from Oregon."

Her smile widens as I walk across the worn linoleum floor past her hospital-style bed. But her eyes stay blank, no lighting up, no widening, no happy crinkling at the corners. I'm relieved that the dark circles under those eyes, so disturbing during my last visit, are gone.

"It's so good to see you, Mom," I say, though I hate this moment, this slap of reality. Mom is gone. Her body is here, but all her memories of time as my mother have vanished. What am I doing here?

I bend down and hug her. As I pull back from the hug and look into her eyes, an aide strides into the room, finds us frozen in this intimate-looking moment, and says in that slight southern accent of lower, slower Delaware, "Who's this, Miss Elsie?"

Mom looks from the aide to me and back again. "He's some relative."

That short, coherent sentence, an accomplishment for her, pains me. Sometimes she tells people I'm her brother, or father, or just a visitor who has to leave now.

I force a smile, turn to the aide, and joke, "I'm her youngest son, Rick. She has another son and daughter but I'm the smartest and best looking."

The aide throws her head back in loud laughter and then asks, "Is that right, Miss Elsie?"

Mom smiles and her eyes shift from the aide to me and back again. Concentration wrinkles appear on her forehead. "Maybe."

The aide offers Mom a cup of juice and a blue pill. "Here you are, Miss Elsie, take this."

Mom puckers her lips, reaches for the pill, and squeezes her eyes shut. As she brings the pill to her mouth, her hand moves this way and that, as if it has a mind of its own. She opens her mouth and drops in the pill. Without upper dentures, her mouth looks like a little cave in a weathered wall. Her other hand trembles as she raises the cup of juice. She makes a face of disapproval but slowly drinks. Drops of orange juice slide down her chin.

Mom hands the aide the empty cup. The aide smiles at her, winks at me, and leaves. I reach for the box of tissues by the chair and wipe Mom's chin. Like a parent with his child.

"How are you?" I ask, though I'm not sure why, given Mom's inability to describe her feelings or physical condition.

"I think ... you should ... put some hair ... on that chair."

Though she's been serving word salad such as this for two years, I'm still not sure how to respond. Ignore, laugh, break down and cry? I take her hand, bring it to my lips, and kiss it, feeling protruding veins and smelling a hint of hand lotion. "That's exactly what we'll do, Mom. We'll put some hair on that chair."

Her eyes widen and she laughs, a sound roughened by age. For a moment I picture her as my younger mom, standing at the ironing board in the dining room, iron in one hand, cigarette in the other, laughing and singing along with the radio and Trini Lopez while I watch mesmerized from between the white upright poles of a stairway banister.

If this woman has Mom's laugh, what else is hidden inside her that she can't reveal? Are there memories, scenes from eighty-six years? Instead of "... put some hair on that chair," maybe she heard inside her head, "I love you, Rick, and I'm so glad to see you." I so wish this is true.

One thing I know for sure: I'm scared to death that I'm closing in on a similar fate, trapped without a past in a body locked into a future. This makes my mortality fears real. It's not just plain vanilla death I fear—it's the possibility of a long, slow disappearance from Alzheimer's that scares me and adds to the pain of watching her descent.

Maybe that's why my incessant journaling in the garden feels so necessary, even desperate. I'm trying to capture moments of my life before they may disappear into the abyss of Alzheimer's.

CHAPTER 19

My Biggest Fear

ON THE NEXT TRIP TO SEE MOM, MARY WENT WITH ME. After that visit, we squeezed into our seats for the long flight to Oregon. The plane had reached cruising altitude when I looked at Mary sitting next to me. Light from the window put her face half in light, half in shadow, like my feelings.

She must have sensed my stare, because she turned to me, read my face, and said, "It's the visit to your mom, right?"

"Yeah, I can't help it. I can't help thinking how sad it is, and how I never want to end up like that."

"It is sad," she said, "but there's no guarantee you'll get Alzheimer's."

"Yeah," I said, "I keep trying to hold on to that. But my memory surely isn't what it once was. Look at how many times you have to tell me about things I forget, how some of the things I forget scare you."

Mary forced out an exasperated breath. "Okay, suppose it did happen. Then what?"

"There's a window, at least there was with Mom, when she knew, we all knew, that her memory was failing."

"Yeah," Mary said, "I remember how frustrated she was when she realized she couldn't do crossword puzzles anymore. And then things got worse."

I pressed my lips together and nodded my head forcefully. "Right. We could see the decline and picture the future, but we never talked about Alzheimer's with her. And I truly regret that." I fell silent, wishing I could change the past. "I would want to talk about it with you once I had a diagnosis and knew where I was heading."

"And then what?"

I forced my head back against the headrest. "Yeah, then what?" I scanned a few seats forward where an inane sitcom flashed silently across the screen of a passenger's laptop. I wished I could escape into someone else's fantasy. "At some point during that window, I'd take control of my life while I still had the mind to make decisions."

Mary drew away from me, pressed against the cabin wall, stayed there as miles slipped away. I said nothing, hoping she would let this conversation die. But that's not Mary. She came close, rested her head on my shoulder, and whispered, "That's not fair. How could you leave me? Why wouldn't you let me take care of you?"

I took her hand and locked onto her blue-gray eyes. Words poured out. "Because there's no guarantee that you're always going to be there. Look, suppose I let you care for me, and I get to where my mom is, and then you're killed in a car accident. Then I'm doomed, left to waste away in a nursing home like her."

"Okay, Rick, calm down." She placed her hand on mine, massaged it gently. "So what would you do?"

As I listened to the hiss of recirculated air, felt the vibration of five hundred miles per hour, an image of how I might end my life flashed through my mind.

Mary bumped her shoulder against mine. "What? Say it."

"I'd load up the backpack, drive to someplace beautiful. Maybe Yellowstone. Maybe hike down to that campsite we had along the Yellowstone River, and never come out."

"You'd do that without me?" Mary asked with a mixture of fear and anger.

My reply, "You could come if you want," felt lame even as I said it.

"And what? Leave you out there in the wilderness? Hike out knowing you're still there?" She stopped, pushed blonde hair behind her ear with her forefinger, maybe picturing the solo hike out. "You've got to be kidding. I don't think I could do that."

I brushed my head against hers, reveled in the softness of her hair, drew in its faint, sweet aroma. "I'm not sure I could either. But I'm clear that I don't want to end up like Mom. That's my biggest fear."

We settled into silence. We'd had this discussion before; we'll have it again. The plane flew on while miles away Mom sat in her stuffed chair behind broken blinds, lost to me, to the world, and maybe to herself.

CHAPTER 20

Genetic Roulette

EVEN WHEN I'M HOME IN OREGON AND NOT CONFRONTED with the reality of Mom, I feel the fear of succumbing to Alzheimer's. That fear is like a low-grade fever that won't go away, a fever I try—and fail—to deny.

After four months of sitting in the garden, I'm finally beginning to see that denial is a doomed approach. Denying fear gives it power over me. So I have decided to face the fear, to research Alzheimer's. Facts might fight or feed the fever, but at least I'll know what I could expect.

After a few hours online, my fear fever spikes. I learn that dementia of the Alzheimer's type (the official name) is the sixth leading cause of death in the US. In 2018 more than 5 million Americans were living with Alzheimer's. By 2050, says the Alzheimer's Association, that number could more than triple to 16 million.

Many of those millions will be baby boomers like me, given the age at which Alzheimer's strikes. That's really no surprise. Just as our oversized cohort has over-whelmed every other phase of life from birthing rooms, to K through 12, to college, to the workplace, we will bury the health-care system with Alzheimer's patients from among our nation's 76 million baby boomers.

The big picture looks bleak, but what about my personal situation: Am I more likely to succumb because Mom passed on a set of genes that makes me more sus-ceptible? Will I lose at genetic roulette?

Though I craved a "no" answer to that question when I started looking for an answer, I had to settle for a "maybe." Researchers have identified a link between the disease and genes on four of a person's forty-six chromosomes. If I inherited a variant of one of those four genes, I am at increased risk of developing late-on-set Alzheimer's, the type that Mom has, the kind that shows up around the time a person turns sixty-five.

But here's the maybe: not everyone with that variant gene gets Alzheimer's, while some without it do. Researchers suspect there are more genes involved as well as nongenetic factors such as education and diet.

Maybe the pain of going back to school at age fifty to obtain a master's in business administration and Mary's obsessive focus on helping me eat well will offset to some degree any renegade genes I have.

Realistically, though, the research reveals that if I'm going to get Alzheimer's, the damage has already started. The disease begins to attack the brain ten to twenty years before symptoms appear. While researchers hope to find a way to prevent the appearance of symptoms, they have not succeeded yet. Once a person starts traveling down the road of cognitive decline, he or she can expect to reach the end of that road within seven to ten years.

After much research, I concluded that the best I can do now is to try to calculate the odds of my following in Mom's footsteps. One study I found showed that the chances of a person like me developing hereditary Alzheimer's are about 1 in 5.

The MBA in me asked, Is 1 in 5 good? Not according to a 2017 list from the National Safety Council. The chances of dying from the big killers on that list, heart disease and cancer, are 1 in 7. Contrast that with dying in a car accident, 1 in 114, or in a plane crash, 1 in 9,821. While those last two make me feel safer flying and driving to see Mom, that 1 in 5 sure feeds my fear fever.

If the odds aren't good, what am I in for? I've watched Mom go through the first two stages, but what about the last? How might the end arrive? I found a book, *How We Die: Reflections on Life's Final Chapter*, that answers that question.

The author, Sherwin Nuland, MD, paints a vivid picture of how I might expire from Alzheimer's. If I don't perish first from a heart attack or stroke, I could gradually lose the ability to chew or swallow my own spit. Trying to feed me could evoke coughing and choking. My loved ones could face the question of whether to insert a feeding tube. Finally, I could reach what Nuland calls a vegetative state. The end would be near, as he graphically describes:

The great majority of people in an Alzheimer's vegetative state will die of some sort of infection, whether it arises in the urinary tract, in the lungs, or in the fetid, bacteria-choked swamp of a bedsore. In the feverish process that ensues, called septicemia, bacteria rush into the bloodstream, rapidly causing shock, cardiac arrhythmias, clotting abnormalities, kidney and liver failure, and death.

Oh, no, I don't want to end my life that way. Nor do I want to put Mary or my family through the countless decisions and constant pain of watching me in a struggle I can't win.

Instead, I'm now even more certain that I would want to choose where, how, and when to die if I lose at genetic roulette and am diagnosed with Alzheimer's.

CHAPTER 21

Misty

NOT TOO LONG AFTER DIGGING INTO ALZHEIMER'S, I'M
back digging in the garden again. As July burns on,
there's little to do but weed, water, and fertilize. I have
just finished all three and settled onto the ground in the
shade of the magnolia tree.

As I sit here, back against the trunk, cooling down,
thinking about Mom and me, Alzheimer's and odds, I
have a vivid recollection of my friend Misty's memorial
service three years ago. Recalling images from that
service, which Misty designed from start to finish,
makes me wonder if designing my memorial service
might help reduce my obsession with death, my focus
on my biggest fear. Wouldn't that be a relief?

Excited, I hurry into the house and sit down in
front of the computer. Music for my memorial service
is a good place—hopefully an easy place—to start. I've
been a singer for most of my adult life. Sometimes while
driving down an open road with a steering wheel for

a drum. Sometimes in a coffee house with a partner who played guitar. Sometimes in an a cappella group with Mary and others. Over those years I found many meaningful songs I love.

But it's not just songs I love. I love being on stage, singing lead, harmonizing, spotting smiles in the front row, feeling a wave of applause. And, really, wouldn't this memorial service be my last performance? Shouldn't I create a set list for my last show? At the very least, shouldn't I assemble a menu of songs that the preparer of my service could choose from?

I click open the computer's music library. On the screen appears a listing of all the songs stored there, about thirteen hundred of them. Surely, somewhere in there are songs I will want played at my memorial service.

To start collecting, I create a new electronic folder and title it SERVICE MUSIC. Fingers hovering just above the keyboard, I lean forward and stare at the letters. Pained by the title, I punch the DELETE key. I type LIFE MUSIC and breathe a sigh of relief.

I look away from the screen and ask myself why I felt relieved when I typed LIFE MUSIC. Perhaps because I seek songs that reveal life's joys and sorrows.

But this collection is for my memorial service. So why delete SERVICE MUSIC? Perhaps because to get to that service I must die.

That thought scares me, but not like the fear from imagining a slow, painful disappearance from Alzheimer's. This memorial service dredges up fears of leaving

Mary, our family, friends, the natural world. It's not the going that scares me; it's the gone.

I sit back and, trying to gain strength to continue, call to mind Misty and her service.

Years ago, Misty, with braided black hair that reached halfway down her back, and her husband, with a bushy auburn beard that hid his neck, were the first to welcome us to their wonderful community of homesteaders and seekers in rural Oregon. My first wife and I had moved to that community to house-sit an off-the-grid cabin.

From that start, we deepened our friendship with Misty, her husband, and their two sons by working, playing, and eating together as years passed and they gave living off the land a go. Even after my wife and I moved to the town of Corvallis, twenty-three miles away, we enjoyed visiting them often.

Years later, Misty and her husband divorced, and she and her sons moved to a small town north of Corvallis. Though I didn't see Misty often, when we ran into each other, the moments sparkled with the magic of old friendship. We'd smile, laugh, even slap a knee and shout for joy as we caught up on intervening months or years.

Eventually Misty remarried and moved to Corvallis, her hair now short and going to gray, her smile still as warm. She became a hospice worker and spent the last decade of her life helping others through the final stages of their lives. She ran weekly meetings to educate and support those grieving the loss of a loved one. She learned how death affects survivors.

Her knowledge wasn't only secondhand. She had survived the all-too-real possibility of dying from cancer. But several years later when cancer returned, this time in her brain, she was told it was terminal. She spent her final months preparing, thinking about what she had seen and heard in weekly grief groups and how her death would hit her husband and two sons. Misty knew she couldn't save them from grief. But she could help them by designing her memorial service. She planned it all: words, music, images, location, guests. She even left space so family members could add touches.

When Mary and I spoke with her adult sons as we left Misty's fine service, they admitted to adding or changing very little. They were thankful their mother had been so thoughtful. They said they had no experience with memorial services, and Misty did a better job than they could have.

Recalling how Misty's courage helped her sons, I command myself to stop cowering and start choosing. As I sample songs, happy and sad, fast and slow, my imagination runs wild. I picture attendees of the service listening to the music and wiping their eyes. Some saying, "That's so Rick." Others exclaiming, "I didn't know he felt that way." I see friends coming forward to share remembrances. I hear laughter and crying. Alone at the computer, clicking the mouse, singing along, I laugh and cry through my virtual memorial service.

Inspired by Misty, I don't quit. I cram nineteen songs into that LIFE MUSIC folder. Their topics run the gamut from boyhood to beyond the grave. Looking over the list, I see that some of the songs even mention heaven and love after death. My heart has been busy.

After picking those songs, I have to stop, though I still need parting words and a slide show of images of important people, places, and times. I don't have the guts to go further today.

I'm not yet ready to meet that bear.

CHAPTER 22

Throwing the Gauntlet

THE PAIN OF PLANNING MY MEMORIAL SERVICE STICKS
with me like the pain of that hot bike tour in Washington and the exhausting climb up South Sister. As
I sagged and doubted on those external adventures, I
sag and doubt in this internal exploration. One week I
face nagging fears about the horrors of Alzheimer's. The
next week I don't have the strength to finish planning
my memorial service. I again wonder if I'm up to the
challenge of exploring the wilds of aging. And again,
the garden mirrors my inner turmoil.

As August arrives, cool-weather plants fade. Sad
kale hangs on with a few leaves atop tattered stalks.
Spinach, compelled by longer days and higher temperatures, has followed nature's instructions to go to seed, to
bolt. The plants didn't grow large enough to harvest. I
planted; they bolted. No eating in between. Lettuce, just
on the edge of bolting, stands taller, light green leaves
slipping slowly from sweet to bitter. The hot-weather

plants—tomato, eggplant, pepper, squash—only hint at growth. In a week or so this garden will look full but there will be little to eat.

In the midst of this transition, I need to start planning the fall and winter garden. This will be my first attempt at off-season gardening. I expect a lot: my goal is to eat from the garden ten months of the year, missing only January and February. The off-season harvest will be greens from plants with unfamiliar names: corn salad, miner's lettuce, Kyoto mizuna. Some of these, according to the seed catalog, will actually grow, not just survive, during winter in the cold frame I built (with, of course, some comments from Dad). The cold frame is a simple wooden structure covered with plastic, four feet square, one and a half feet tall, with a slanted lid. I hope it will provide a suitable winter microclimate.

Sitting here amid transition, warmed by morning sun, it's hard to imagine harvesting greens all winter, hard to imagine planning the memorial service. All I can envision is how these challenges will stretch me. All I can say is, "Can I do this?"

And that's good. Eventually asking that question was the goal Mary and I wanted to reach on each of our last seven summer adventures.

———

We would begin planning a summer adventure as the winter wind splattered cold rain against our bedroom window. Below that window we nested in bed, snuggled under a down comforter, coffee cups steaming on bedside tables. Books, maps, and printouts spread across the bed-covers and tantalized two souls hungry for adventure. We had the time to debate destinations, to ruminate on whether to hike or bike. We also had the energy, since we had not started the intense exercise regimen of late spring and early summer. We were relaxed and confident.

As we sat in bed, we scanned the books and print-outs for hiking trails and bike routes with descriptions such as "challenging," "for the serious hiker," or "for the cyclist who loves hills." We did this because we were planning an adventure, not a vacation. On an adventure we crave unknowns, seek an experience that will compel us to eventually ask, "Can we do this?"

Setting ourselves up for challenges could get out of hand, though, because we are both competitive. When one of us found a challenging hike or bike ride, the other tried to beat it. That happened every year; we never grew immune.

That's how we decided to challenge ourselves two summers ago with not just a four-hundred-mile self-supported bike tour through hilly northwest Montana. Oh, no, that wasn't enough. We would follow it with a five-day hike under full pack, deep into the mountainous backcountry of Glacier National Park.

I don't remember which one of us said, "Let's go backpacking in Glacier after the bike tour." Or which one of us cooed, "Ooh, yeah, that'll be a challenge!" It didn't matter; the gauntlet was thrown.

CHAPTER 23

Lightning, Thunder, Snow

ON THE THIRD DAY OF THAT BACKPACK INTO GLACIER, WE stood after dinner and watched clouds rush our way, countless waves of gray and purple. A storm was heading for our tent in the tenuous shelter of ragged timberline at 7,200 feet. A cold wind slapped our tent, making it shudder.

"Do you want to build a wall on the windward side of the tent?" I asked.

"You bet!" Mary yelped, and we hustled toward the tent, each picking up a large rock from a nearby rubble field. We scurried back and forth between the rubble and the tent, building a rough wall. Until lightning flashed nearby.

Mary looked in the direction of the lightning and then at the wall, half as high as the tent. "Well, it's better than nothing," she said.

Without another word, we scooted into the tent and zipped it shut. Inside, it was almost peaceful. Until we heard a gust rumbling toward us and wind slammed the tent, bending the fabric inward. So much for the protection of the rock wall.

Rain began to pelt the tent. I knelt on my sleeping bag and jammed loose clothing and gear into protective plastic bags.

Mary slipped into her sleeping bag, cinched the bag's hood tight around her head, and asked, "Do you want to read to each other?"

I nodded, finished packing, put on my headlamp, and pulled out a book containing essays on wildfire. It seemed especially poignant to add the element of fire to the water and wind nature was delivering. I handed the book to Mary.

Just as she was about to start reading aloud, the rain and wind stopped. In the silence, we looked at each other.

"Uh oh," I said.

Lightning flashed, brighter than our headlamps, even through the tent wall.

I silently counted the seconds between flash and thunder and said aloud, "Ten." We knew that since sound travels at about 1,100 feet per second, the lightning was just two miles away. Too close.

When Mary started reading aloud about the rampage of a massive wildfire, I watched white clouds of her breath billow into her headlamp's beam.

"Did you feel it just get colder?" I asked.

"Yeah, the temperature's dropping like a stone!" she said.

Then something new pummeled the tent.

"That sounds like hail," I said. Lightning flashed. I counted. "Five. A mile. Coming closer."

"Are you getting scared?" Mary asked.

"Yeah! Rain and wind I can handle, but lightning at timberline ..." I let the thought drift away with my misty breath.

Mary continued reading where she had left off. I snuggled deep into my sleeping bag, thrilled by the author's words inside the tent and frightened by the power of nature outside.

When she finished the essay, we turned off our headlamps and let darkness and the storm engulf us. For the next three hours I tried, but failed, to sleep. Just after midnight, I unzipped my bag. Inside the tent felt unusually warm. I sat up and the top of my head brushed against the tent's sagging ceiling. I pushed my hand against the ceiling and felt snow slide down the side.

"Look at this!" I said, shaking Mary awake and turning on my headlamp. As she groaned and turned toward me with her hand shading her eyes, I jostled the tent wall by her head. With a whoosh and thud, more snow slid. "We've got some tent cleaning to do."

We dressed and climbed out into snow that was driven by wind straight across the bobbling beams of our headlamps. Using one of my sandals like a small snow shovel, I slid snow off one side of the tent. Mary cleared the other.

We crawled back in, undressed, and slid into our bags. For two more hours, as sleep eluded, we discussed challenging scenarios: Should we stay here if we can't find the trail in the morning because the snow is too deep? If we stay, will we have enough food and fuel for the rest of the trip? Should we try to hike out, looking for a snow-covered trail with only map and compass to guide us? With these unknowns, we finally arrived at the big question—Can we do this? Our hike has become an adventure.

We managed about three hours' sleep before pastel daylight woke us. We lay in our bags listening to wind rustling trees and the satisfying sound of nothing hitting the tent. Mary slithered out of her bag, peered outside, and exclaimed, "Whoa, buddy, winter got here last night!"

Indeed, it had. The snow that had scared us awake now covered the basin in a six-inch-thick blanket. We climbed out to see if the return trail was visible. It was and we applauded. We were just 1,000 vertical feet above a lake surrounded by green. In that green—and just a few miles away—was our next campsite. We can do this!

CHAPTER 24

Companion Planting

T<small>HAT SNOWSTORM TRANSFORMED A HIKE IN THE WILDS</small> of Glacier into an adventure. And I have arrived at a similar point in exploring the wilds of aging. By asking, "Can I do this?" this sitting in the garden has become an adventure and that excites me.

When I started this internal adventure, my body was exhausted. Now, after five restful months, I'm reenergizing. Some days I can picture going on a multiday bike tour next spring. But what will my aging body be ready for? How physically demanding a tour should I design? Accepting that a decline in physical ability accompanies aging, I will need to match future tours with future capacities. Otherwise, I could end up in this garden visiting my paper therapist again.

I talked recently about this balancing act with a silver-haired neighbor who is twenty years older—and far wiser—than me. And still physically active. He grinned and confided that although future adventures will be less physically demanding than past ones, I would enjoy them as much. "Enjoyment doesn't decline with age," he said with a chuckle.

Today I have a chance to gauge the shape my reenergized body is in. My riding partner Jim has invited Mary and me to join him and his wife, Janet, and cycle to the 4,000-foot summit of Mary's Peak, the highest point in Oregon's Coast Range. I'm glad Jim invited me since I recently told him I would not be going on the two-week bike tour in the Canadian Rockies that he and I had considered. He said he was disappointed but understood when I confessed that I was not yet feeling motivated for a long, mountainous tour.

Once we start pedaling up Mary's Peak, I remember this is not an easy ride. Our route to the top is twenty-five miles, almost all climbing, the last ten miles very steep. After three and a half hours, as I struggle through the steep section with Jim and Janet ahead and Mary behind, I sing in my head—over and over—a line from an old Rolling Stones' song: "This could be the last time . . ."

I'm happy to stop when Jim suggests lunch beside a roadside waterfall that tumbles down past ferns and drops into a pool that has been enclosed with a low wall of natural rock. I step off my bike and enjoy the cooling mist from the falls.

When Mary arrives, her face is nearly the color of her red helmet. "Phew, I could turn around right here," she gasps. She dismounts, stands unsteadily, and removes her helmet, revealing hair fashioned by sweat into a style she calls helmet head.

I grab Mary's shoulders, look into her eyes, and admit, "I could turn around right here too! For the past mile or so I've been wondering if this is the last time I'll ever do this ride."

Mary breaks eye contact and tilts her head away from me. Jim looks over at us and frowns. I sense disapproval from both.

"I'm really hungry, just feeling totally out of energy," she says, pulling away from my grip and turning toward her bike. "I could sure use some food." She digs our lunch out of her saddle bag and walks toward the waterfall.

Jim stomps over and thrusts his sweaty, six-foot-two-inch body toward me. He frowns and growls, "I'm not happy with you."

His height (he's six inches taller than I am), look, and tone intimidate me. "For what?" I ask.

"All this talk about getting older and how your body's changing. Talking about not going to the top today. Hey, I'm sixty-six and I'm going!" He shakes his head in dismay. "Why wouldn't you want to do this? I just don't get it!"

I don't know what to say. I've not seen Jim growl in the six years I've known him. And I'm confused; he didn't growl when I backed out of the Canadian Rockies tour.

Jim mutters, "Maybe we'll all feel better after lunch." He turns and walks away.

The four of us grunt and groan as we sit down with our lunches on the wall by the waterfall. There's little conversation, and I wonder what Mary is feeling. But now doesn't seem to be the time to ask. Instead, I refresh myself in silence with the crackers, cheese, and grapes that Mary and I share.

Once finished, the four of us start to pack up. We have three more steep miles before the summit.

"Man, I could really enjoy a nap," I say through a yawn. "But I think I'm willing to give the peak a try."

"Let's go then," Jim says, smiling and slapping me on the back, more like the friend I've come to know after years of touring together.

While Jim and Mary chat and pack, Janet and I depart, riding beside one another into a tunnel of trees. At the summit, Janet and I emerge into the brightness of a parking lot. When Mary and Jim arrive, we slap high-fives and take a brief rest. Then we don our jackets in preparation for the ride's reward, a screaming descent.

Jim—the downhill lover—leads, and I chase him through twists and turns. The wind buffets me as I lightly tap the brakes and lean into a curve at about thirty-five miles per hour. I'm happy to be going with gravity instead of fighting it. So is Jim; I hear his joyous whoop as he accelerates into another turn.

———

I have calculated that Jim and I have logged more than fifteen hundred miles bike touring together, often up and down mountain roads like Mary's Peak. Now I realize that my decision to slow down, to take this solo internal adventure, may feel to him like the loss of an adventure companion.

In gardening there's a theory called companion planting. Some plants like each other and grow better when planted side by side. The theory goes, for example, that pole beans and corn are companions and grow better together.

Jim and I are like companion plants. Five years ago when we set out on our first-ever tour to follow the mountainous Lewis and Clark trail for seven hundred miles, we planted ourselves side by side in life's garden of adventures. We thrived in each other's presence: challenged one another to push on when we felt empty, lifted the other's spirits when the road wore them down, and helped each other talk through life's troubles.

After that first tour there were many more days of side-by-side training and touring. With each ride our companionship grew deeper and stronger.

But now, for all Jim knows, our days of adventuring together are over. Though my decision feels right for me, my absence leaves him wilting without an adventure partner.

A pang of guilt cuts through me as I realize that I have left my companion with a void that may be hard to fill.

CHAPTER 25

Hard Questions

THE IMAGE OF JIM'S SWEATING, GROWLING FACE HAUNTS me. So does the disapproval I sensed from Mary that day when I admitted to her that ride might be the last I make to the top of Mary's Peak. She and I haven't discussed her feelings about that statement, and I wonder what she felt then and feels now. I also think I might not want to know. I've taken the safe route and not pried.

A couple of weeks after that tough climb, Mary sits across from me at the green metal patio table nestled in the shade of our backyard magnolia. Colorful dishes from tonight's dinner dot the tabletop on this fine August evening. While we ate that dinner, Mary was unusually quiet, and that troubled me.

Now, Mary, still quiet, leans back in her chair, turns her head to the right, and stares where the setting sun's rays paint our backyard trees orange. She nods her head once as if having made a decision. She faces me and says, "I don't understand why you're choosing to focus so much on death rather than life." She stops, stares into my eyes. "It feels a bit like self-pity. After all, you could have twenty or thirty years yet to live." She clasps her arms across her black fleece top; her lips shape a determined frown. "To stop adventuring when you have a perfectly healthy body makes no sense to me."

I lean in toward the table, push away my empty plate and say, "I know that it must have shocked you when I said I was done adventuring. It surprised me too. But I felt like I just needed to stop."

"I'll say it *surprised* me!" Mary declares. "It surprised our friends too! It's like you just flipped a switch. One minute you're adventuring," she flicks her hand as if smacking a wall switch, "and the next you're *done.* And I *still* don't get why you want to stop *completely.*"

"I think I'm starting to figure that out. Those deaths just gutted my sense of immortality, really rocked me to my core. Then last summer's hiking and biking left me believing my body needed to stop. I ended that summer feeling old and scared instead of happy and rejuvenated."

Mary throws her right hand in the air and says forcefully, "But you're *not* old! You're only *sixty-one*, for God's sake." As her words bounce off the house and back to us, she looks past me and says gently, "And I don't think that stopping adventuring is good for you. I think that telling yourself you need to stop will age you, really slow you down."

"That's a good point," I say with a nod and lean back

into my chair to consider it. I've told Mary many times over the years how careful I am with self-talk, that self-talk can be self-fulfilling. Telling myself I'm limited in some way—even if that's not actually true—can make me act limited. "Well, I sure don't want to self-talk my way into becoming old and finished with adventuring."

"So what are you going to do?" Mary asks. "I still want to adventure. *I'm* not ready to stop." She looks down and rubs her palms along the sleeves of her top. "Hell, I'll be retiring too in less than a year, and we had all these great ideas for adventures. It's like we paved the way for them, and you've pulled the rug right out from under us."

Guilt jolts me. While I needed to stop adventuring, I don't want to be the one keeping Mary and me from experiences that have brought us such joy. I don't want her to feel—as I think Jim might—the frustration of losing an adventure companion.

But at the same time, I feel frustrated: Mary and Jim are struggling to let me be who I need to be right now. They don't want me to stop adventuring, but I don't feel I can continue. Yet I trust them; they've faced many challenges with me. They know what I can do. And maybe they have a point. Perhaps I reacted too strongly by telling them last March—seemingly out of nowhere—that my days of adventuring were over, that I was done.

I try not to sound defensive as I say to Mary, "I think that those deaths made me realize that no matter how well I take care of myself, I can't control the fact that I could die any day. And that scared me."

I lean my head back, stare into the shiny, dark green foliage of the magnolia, think about Jana, Misty, Daniel, Mammaw. A small flock of birds arrives, chirping, darting from branch to branch. Then, as quickly as they arrived, they depart, leaving only a memory of motion.

I look at Mary and say, "I think I needed to come to grips with accepting my mortality before I could move on."

"Well, have you?" she asks, squinting with understandable exasperation.

Mary accepted her mortality years ago, at age forty, when she was diagnosed with cancer, when she battled a real killer. All these years later we still breathe a sigh of relief when she gets the green light after a visit to her oncologist.

On that level, my situation doesn't compare. But there is no doubt that facing aging and dying twisted me into a knot, led me into an important phase of floundering, searching, and accepting.

I look at Mary and say, "Yeah, I think I've come to grips with the obvious fact that I'll one day die. And that I'll decline physically as I age."

"So," she asks, "are you done with sitting in this garden?"

"Not yet. I still feel the need to dig deeper."

"You're *not* done? When do you think you *will* be?"

Mary's hard questions have helped me make other decisions in my life, and now they've done it again.

"I want to give this a full year. I started sitting in the garden in March, and a year would take me to next spring. I really like the idea of four seasons in the garden, and what I can learn in a year of journaling. So far I've figured out what stopped me, but I don't yet know where I'm heading." I pause and rub my hand against the stubble on my chin, thinking about upcoming months. "I wonder how I'll be different after the year is over."

"Oh, you'll be different. You're *different* now. But do you think you might be open to some adventuring after the year ends?" Mary asks with a hopeful smile.

"My energy has started to come back, and since our Mary's Peak ride I've thought about a bike tour with Jim next spring, while I wait for you to retire in June."

"Oh, really. Where?"

"Death Valley. The weather should be good. And that seems like a fitting spot for celebrating the end of this year." I grin as I catch the irony of *Death* Valley.

Mary erupts in loud laughter. "That is *so you*." She slaps her hand on the metal table and the dishes bounce and rattle.

My laughter mingles with hers, filling the backyard.

CHAPTER 26

Unblazed Trail

A WEEK HAS PASSED SINCE THE BACKYARD CONFRONTA-tion with Mary. In addition to telling her that I will limit my internal adventure to a year, I've told Jim and others that I'm not done with external adventuring. These public announcements of a finish line strengthen my commitment to this private journey.

With an end point in the distance, I'm excited about what will happen during the next six months of reflect-ing and writing. Though I'm much more accepting of my aging, physical decline, and mortality, there are still unknowns to explore: imagining my deathbed, planning a memorial service, deciding about afterlife.

There's much uncertainty; I'm not sure where I'll end up. I can't see much more than a faint, unblazed trail to follow. For some people a trail with no markers might be one to avoid. But I know from a hike in Yel-lowstone that sometimes the unblazed trail can be the most rewarding.

The second day of that hike deep into Yellowstone's backcountry started well. When Mary and I climbed out of the cold hollow where we had camped, the warming sun inspired us to meander in silence. Until we saw the first grizzly track. Then we started taking turns shouting "Yo Bear!"—especially when the trail threaded through head-high ripe berry patches thick enough to hide a gang of snacking bears.

A couple of anxious hours later we reached a junction on the edge of a large golden meadow where we would leave Yellowstone and enter Gallatin National Forest. We had to choose between two trails. We took turns looking across the meadow through binoculars, trying to locate the one we wanted, the shorter one. We couldn't find it.

We discussed the warning we had received from a backcountry ranger: each year they have to rescue hikers in this area. Perhaps because hikers took faint trails like the one we sought. We decided to take the trail we could see, the longer one.

We moved out and felt secure hiking along what looked like an old jeep road. But as the road shrank to a single track, our sense of security dwindled with it. After about a mile, we had to step off the trail to let pass a string of pack horses carrying a few tourists. We asked the guide bringing up the rear whether the connecting trail we hoped to find ahead was marked.

He pulled off his Stetson, wiped his brow with his

sleeve, and said, "Yup, that trail's there. It's even got a little sign." With his hands he portrayed a sign the size of a piece of notebook paper. "But it ain't much of a trail. Hell, it's even narrower than this one." He put his hat on, nodded farewell, and left.

Continuing on, we found the small sign, stopped, and studied our map. This connector trail would eventually reach the more heavily used Hellroaring Creek trail and our campsite for the night. Heading down the connector, we soon realized that the guide was right; in places the trail was only as wide as my boot. I stopped looking down to try to find the trail. Instead, I scanned ahead where the indistinct trail appeared like a faint, squiggly black line on a rough green canvas.

Since the trail was unblazed, had no orange markers mounted head high on trailside trees, I regularly pulled out the map and searched for an upcoming landmark such as a stream crossing or sharp bend. I then gave Mary an estimate of the time by which we should reach that feature. Each time we hit the mark, we cheered.

After four hours of trail finding in ninety-degree heat, we picked our way down a half mile of rocky switchbacks toward Hellroaring Creek. Tired, hungry, thirsty, and relieved to now be able to follow a blazed trail, we stumbled along until we found a stream bank with soft grass and cool shade, a perfect lunch spot. I collapsed on the bank and started pulling together our meal. Mary slid down the bank to refill our water containers. After lunch we packed up and hiked on, our stiff bodies complaining.

As the afternoon and miles wore on, our pace slowed. We were plodding along a poorly blazed trail through dense forest and again shouting "Yo Bear!" by the time we reached the sign indicating we were reentering Yellowstone.

When we stopped in the middle of the trail for a break, I told Mary that our next landmark would be a short side trail to our campsite. We let out a cheer and moved on. As the time to reach the side trail arrived but the side trail did not, our anxiety and fatigue increased. We examined the map and decided we weren't lost; I had just underestimated the distance we had to cover. We pushed on and found the side trail. When we finally stepped into the campsite, a drizzle arrived out of nowhere. We rushed to set up the tent.

After dinner, we climbed in the tent and burrowed deep into our bags, feet sore and nerves frayed. And pleased with how we had succeeded at following an unblazed trail.

———

Like that Yellowstone hike, the trail I will follow for the rest of this internal adventure is hard to see. Unlike that hike, I don't have a map. Though I'm determined and motivated, determination and motivation without a map can simply mean I get lost quicker.

But each session reflecting and writing in the garden provides a bit of trail finding. Something comes up; I follow it. Today it was uncertainty. Next could be joy, sorrow, or anything in between. Each journal entry leads me forward, creates another blaze along the trail.

And I want to keep moving; there's much yet to discover. As I would for an external adventure, I need to look outside myself for direction. Many others have explored aging, mortality, and afterlife. Though some of their discoveries and revelations may not resonate with me completely, many will act as blazes along my trail.

And just like during that Yellowstone hike, I want to reach a spot where I sleep well, happy that I left the known; overcame fear, vulnerability, and uncertainty; and took the unblazed trail into the wilds of aging.

CHAPTER 27

Nature Nurture

OVER THE LAST MONTH, I'VE TRAVELED AN UNBLAZED gardening trail as well, by planting my first fall garden. Now, the miner's lettuce, corn salad, and Kyoto mizuna are in various stages of growth: tiny sprouts just arching out of the ground, inch-high starts with first true leaves, and six-inch-tall beauties, green and ready for thinning.

Watching the garden sprout, I've thought about how seeds respond to their environment. I've thought about nature versus nurture.

The seeds I planted for those fall greens are tiny, smaller than grains of cracked black pepper. Yet each minuscule seed contains all the instructions necessary to produce a full-sized plant. That's nature. But you must plant them at the proper depth in a spot with the right amount of sunlight, give them enough water, keep the slugs and deer away, and fertilize. That's nurture.

The nature-nurture concept can also be applied to people. I first heard that argument when I was in

an undergraduate psychology class. We debated passionately about the relative importance of nature and
nurture in a person's development. Do children grow
from tiny seeds into the adults they become because of
the nature of their genes or because of the nurturing of
parents, siblings, grandparents, and other caregivers?

After decades as a counselor and parent, I'm in the
nurture camp. Early nurturing points us in certain life
directions, down certain paths. We can meet others later
who influence us for better or worse. And sometimes
we make individual—and often painful—decisions that
can change, ruin, or save our lives.

Dad was an alcoholic. I'm told that for many years his
drinking was not a problem; he simply enjoyed his
beer. But when life's pressures grew too strong, he used
alcohol to cope. From the time I was fifteen to seventeen, I was the only family member living with him.
My parents had divorced, and my mother, sister, and
brother had moved to Delaware.

I chose to stay in Baltimore with Dad because I didn't
want to move to a new high school. I didn't want to lose
old friends or have to make new ones. While that made
teenager sense as far as my social life was concerned, I
had no idea what I was in for by staying with Dad.

At first, living alone with him was like living with
a stranger. He *was* a stranger. When my brother, sister,
and I were growing up, none of us had spent much

time with him. Dad was rarely at home. He had always worked two jobs, trying to make ends meet. When he was home, he was usually asleep on the couch.

In the months after the divorce, I was shocked to see his drinking grow progressively worse, advancing from having a couple of beers in our apartment in the evening to coming home drunk at all hours any night of the week. I wondered how he kept his job. I worried about him and sometimes found myself coming to the rescue when he lost control. One memorable mission, when I was nearly seventeen, tops the list.

CHAPTER 28

The Crystal Ball

ON THAT MEMORABLE NIGHT, A SCHOOL NIGHT AROUND 10 p.m., when Dad still had not come home from work, I sighed and put the prepackaged dinner I had fixed for him in the refrigerator. I sat on the couch, looking at but not seeing the show on the TV. When I couldn't stand wondering where he was anymore, I left our apartment and got into the old clunker he had bought before all the money went for booze. I searched for him at two neighborhood taverns our family had frequented on weekends to play shuffleboard and eat dinner. No luck.

Increasingly anxious, I drove around aimlessly, wondering where to go next. I could only think of one place, but the thought of going there alone at night scared me. The Crystal Ball Inn was on Route 40, a once important highway that now bisected a dying commercial district containing the bar, a half-empty used car lot, a run-down motel, and a dimly lit diner.

When I was younger, Dad had occasionally taken

me to the Crystal Ball on weekend afternoons. Even in the light of day with the front door propped open with a brick, the bar reeked of cigarette smoke and spilled beer. The jukebox blared country and western music. I would sit beside him at the bar, sipping a soft drink, eating salty pistachios or spicy beef jerky. Occasionally we would talk, but mostly I watched him smoke, drink beer, and slam shots of whiskey or shoot pool with a group of guys from his job. Sometimes they would let me play; I enjoyed their attention and kidding as I lost.

Having never been to the Crystal Ball at night, I wasn't sure what to expect. Dad had once told me that on any given night a fight could erupt. As I drove up to the bar, I worried that maybe he had been hurt in a brawl, though he wasn't a fighting drunk. I wondered if I would see anyone I knew who could help me.

I parked the car as close to the building as I could, got out, and pulled open the bar's big front door. The clacking of pool balls smashed into the loud chorus of a country and western song. I stepped inside and pressed myself into the shadows along a wall. I looked around, hoping to see Dad. He wasn't with the men clustered under the fluorescent light shining on the pool table. He wasn't seated at the bar. He wasn't anywhere I could see. And I sure wasn't going to sneak around looking for him.

Disappointed, I snuck to the bar where Crystal, the owner, was working. I waved to get the attention of this tough older woman, face covered with makeup, lips painted fiery red, dyed black hair teased high. She smiled and approached. I asked if she had seen my dad.

She turned to pull a draft beer and said over her shoulder, "Oh, yeah, Hon, haven't I ever."

I glanced again around the dimly lit room. "Well, where is he?"

She served the draft to a tired-looking man in dirty work clothes roosting on a barstool beneath a cloud of cigarette smoke. Then she looked at me and said, "He went off with the Jones twins to Sherrie's Show Bar downtown."

Oh, no, not the Jones twins. They worked with Dad and were younger and wilder and notorious for causing trouble. And Sherrie's was the last place I wanted to go. It was like so many of the bars on Baltimore's nearby Block—the infamous row of strip joints signed with gaudy neon women kicking up long legs. When I was growing up just outside the city limits, a teenage rite of passage had been to cruise the Block with friends, fantasizing about what went on in those joints. But going to a strip joint alone, looking for Dad? That was another story.

"Sherrie's?" I asked, hoping she would give a different answer.

"Yeah, Hon, that's where you'll find your old man." She leaned across the bar toward me, her big hands working a damp towel. "And I think he'll need a ride." She ended her whisper with a wink and went to tend to a customer.

I left the bar and got in my car, started the engine, and drove toward Sherrie's, worried about what I would do when I arrived. Once there and still unsure, I found a parking spot in front of the bar and sat behind the wheel talking aloud to myself. "I'm not old enough to go in there. How do I find him even if I get in?" I banged the steering wheel with my fist and listened to the big wheel vibrate. I hit the wheel again and then shouted, "Why do I have to do this?"

Finally, I stepped out, slammed the car door, and approached the entrance of the club with its NO MINORS ALLOWED sign. I pounded on the door, and a face appeared in a narrow eye-level window. The door opened, and a man, shorter than me but much broader, stood blocking the entrance. His dark hair was combed straight back and shiny with oil. His nose and cheeks were red. From his pants zipper hung a one-foot-square pink plastic padlock. I stared at it and considered running back to the car.

A thick cloud of cigarette smoke rolled out the door, and I felt myself choking as I inhaled.

The man looked at me, then up and down the street. "And what would you be wanting, Boy?" he said, his Irish accent forceful.

"My dad," I said, looking past the man into the bar with its shadows, flashing colored lights, and rhythmic drum.

"And who would he be?" he smirked.

I looked down, past the padlock to his shiny black

shoes. I didn't want to use our last name, didn't want this guy to know it. I looked at him and said softly, "Ben."

"Ben, is it?" He threw his hands up in the air and barked, "You'll have to tell me more than that, Boy."

I stepped back and debated leaving again. But instead I stood my ground and said, "Red hair, my size, came here with two guys who are twins."

"Oh, the Jones boys," he said, nodding. "They left a while ago, but he's still here." Then gentler: "Come along, Boy. We'll get him."

I followed the Irishman into the crowded bar filled with men, some sitting in dark corners beside big-breasted dancers in skimpy outfits. The stage, now empty, was a splash of white light through a fog of smoke. I stuck very close as he steered between tables and chairs.

We found my father, alone, slumped forward, head down on a table overflowing with full ashtrays and empty beer and shot glasses. My worry for Dad's safety turned to disgust at his appearance.

We pulled him to his feet; he put up no resistance but sure didn't help. He mumbled nonsense as we hauled him to the car, the Irishman on one side, me on the other. After we poured him into the front seat, I scooted around to the driver's side, got in, locked my door, and let slip a quiet sigh of relief.

The Irishman rolled down Dad's window before gently closing that door. Then he leaned through the window and said almost tenderly, "He's a good man. Been coming here for years. Something's wrong at home, I fancy." He patted my father's shoulder, turned, and walked back to the club. His plastic lock clunked with each step.

That guy knows my Dad?

I looked at my father—eyes closed, mouth open, head against the window. I started the car and drove toward home.

CHAPTER 29

Facing Down Alcohol

TWENTY YEARS LATER, I WAS HOME—IN RURAL OREGON— lying on my back across the bed in our master bedroom, crying. I had retreated to the bedroom after Mom had called and told me that Dad had just died of alcohol-related problems. My wife was in town on errands. Our four-year-old daughter, Allison, was snuggled in a blanket in the living room, watching a video.

Sniffling, sobbing, my right arm across my forehead, I was thinking about fathers, children, and alcohol.

After dragging Dad out of Sherrie's Show Bar, I went on to graduate from high school in Baltimore. Right after that I enlisted in the army and spent two years overseas in an alcohol fog, never once considering that drinking was a dangerous path. Upon returning from my tour, I drank regularly and sometimes to excess with friends as I completed college. As the years passed, I drank less, but alcohol stayed in my life. While I never called myself an alcoholic, I knew that alcohol still had a strong pull on me—as it had on Dad.

Could that pull be genetic? Would I succumb like he did if life got too rough? Worse yet, had I passed this craving on to Allison?

Lying on the bed, sandwiched between grief for my dad and fear for my daughter, I was unaware that Allison had slipped into the bedroom until her small hand caressed my forehead. I turned on my side and looked into her loving eyes. "Hey, you," I said and pulled her up onto the bed beside me.

She hugged me and buried her face in my flannel shirt. Her muffled words vibrated my chest, "It'll be all right, Dad. I love you."

A fresh wave of tears poured forth, and I thought: *I never want you to have to rescue me. I never want you to be embarrassed by me. And I never want to teach you to be an alcoholic.*

I didn't say any of those words. I just held her small body, smelled her warm brown hair. Perhaps in the strongest way ever, I experienced the responsibility of being a father, of nurturing a child.

Later that the evening when I was the only one awake, I walked to the refrigerator, craving a snack. I opened the door, squatted, and saw four cans of beer. I reached for one, thinking it would help me relax. Then I recalled my unspoken promise to Allison. I grabbed the four beers, tiptoed outside, and dropped them one by one into the trash. I looked at Allison's dark window, nodded my head, smiled, and walked back inside.

———

Now, sitting in the garden, staring at September's tiny greens, thinking about nature and nurture, I calculate that twenty-four years have passed since Dad died and I quit drinking.

Even now there are times when the thought of a cold beer tempts me. That's nature.

But I've resisted the urges. Allison has never had to rescue me. Nor does she have a problem with alcohol. That's nurture.

But as I sit here, feeling again the relief of facing down alcohol, I can't help but wonder: Why has Dad appeared again? What is the message in this memory?

I look around at the garden and recall why I've chosen to sit here and write.

The message arrives: If I can face something as strong as alcohol, I can face aging, declining, and mortality. If I can nurture a child, I can nurture myself through this internal adventure.

CHAPTER 30

Fall of the Career

HIGH GRAY CLOUDS TUMBLE NORTHWARD. THE ONLY evidence of the morning sun is a bright jagged crack between two clumps of clouds. The smell of moist bark mulch fills the air, a reminder of last night's heavy rain. The flower bed that fills the center of our garden—the bed we call the Riot Garden when in bloom because of its abundant colors, shapes, and sizes—is now well past blooming and looks like the aftermath of an actual riot. Fall's returning rain has beaten and bent the plants. The crocosmia that enticed hummingbirds with their brilliant redness for the last four months are now topped by dead blossoms; their leaves a mix of yellow and green variegated death.

The fall planting in Mammaw's Garden that started strong has stalled. The prospects for fall harvest don't look good. For winter they look worse. This is the first week of October and the low sun, even when due south, only illuminates an area in the garden the width of a bowling lane. Few greens receive direct sun. While this is obvious to me now, a more experienced gardener would have pictured this earlier and designed and planted accordingly.

The bright red tomato on the Early Girl looks like the last bulb on a fading Christmas tree, a reminder of happier times. I'm inclined to pull the plant and put it out of my misery. I have pulled the dying green beans, but their skeletons still cling to a trellis and haunt the beds.

There's little here to inspire. It's time to close down the deteriorating garden and head inside until the soil warms enough to sprout the first greens of spring.

As I sit here, lamenting the end of the growing season and the coming of winter, I find myself thinking about the end of my career and the coming of retirement. Once again the garden reflects my inner turmoil.

———

Eighteen months ago—well before I retreated to the garden—I sat in my home office at 5 a.m. reading and highlighting passages in a multi-page memo from the owners of the small company that employs me to provide vocational rehabilitation to injured workers. The window by my desk was a dark mirror, reflecting my frowning face, a steaming first cup of coffee, and the white pages of the memo bright against a dark cherry desktop. The owners, Grace and Coleen, had written this memo to prepare us for a company-wide retreat at which we would decide how to deal with the steep decline in our business.

After two decades with this company I had advanced through every job in the profession's career ladder, gaining responsibility in each step from entry-level to management. Along the way and on my own, I had written a book on job search, consulted on a book about the impact of job loss, and hosted a public radio series about the ins and outs, the joys and sorrows of working and not working.

Though I had made a good living and prospered longer than many of my colleagues, those golden days were disappearing for me and for the company. As statistics in the memo revealed, over the last year half our consultants had left the company and maybe the profession as their workloads and incomes shrank. The rest of us hung on while earning less.

I turned away from the memo's harsh numbers and pressed the coffee cup against my cheek, felt its soothing warmth. I looked out the window at a hint of morning sun on the gray bark of the tall Douglas fir that shades our hammock. I realized that the owners had no good news; their honest and painful statistics were intended to kick-start us survivors into facing even more challenging changes.

Though I preferred to deny or ignore, I put down the coffee cup and forced my attention back to the memo. Flipping a page, I highlighted the owners' real message: "For us to go forward, it appears we need to redefine our services and ourselves."

Bridling at the idea of redefining myself with

retirement on the horizon, I crumpled the memo, threw it to the floor, stood, and stomped on it again and again. I picked up the coffee cup, inhaled its aroma, took a sip, and said aloud with as much disgust as I was feeling, "Why bother?"

As I looked out the window again and watched the night's shadows disappear, replaced by the soft clarity of morning light, one passage in the memo kept running through my head. Sighing, I reached down, retrieved the memo, placed it on the desktop, and smoothed it as much as I could. I flipped a wrinkled page, ran my finger down the next page, and stopped at a paragraph I had highlighted in which the owners described the transition we could expect. "Largely, this includes a substantial period of time in the unknown ... It also includes the opportunity to try new ways to use skills, open doors for ongoing work options ..."

Their description of redefining myself at work sounded just like how I pictured redefining myself in retirement. I knew I was finished with redefining, recreating, searching for a new niche, building a new customer base, however you want to describe the struggle to earn a buck in a constantly changing workplace. If I recreated myself, it would be as a retiree, finding a new passion that challenged me—perhaps exploring and learning about Yellowstone or some other wild land.

I dropped the memo back into the trashcan.

A week later I drove to the company retreat. When

the first session began, Grace and Coleen launched right into the retreat's purpose. They described four areas we could pursue to diversify and increase business. Though I halfheartedly considered the options, none interested me.

When the session ended, we filed silently into an adjoining room for lunch. I made a point of sitting with Grace and Coleen. I thanked them for making my life easy and profitable all these years by keeping the company going through good and bad times—no small feat. I told them about my plans to retire come hell or high water on the day I turned sixty-two. Each got a wistful look in her eyes and said she wished she could do the same.

I then said that I was not going to try to redefine myself. I also assured them that I would not stand in the way of change, would not be a curmudgeon or naysayer. With that discussion, I charted my course for the next year and a half. I would ride the horse in the direction it was going even if that meant the death of my career.

———

Now, eighteen months later, I'm sitting in my garden retreat, just weeks from retiring. As expected, without any efforts to reinvent myself, my caseload has dried up, my earnings have plummeted. The work phone rarely rings; the e-mail in-box is often empty.

Sometimes when that silent phone screams at me or that empty in-box fills me with regret, I get angry at myself for refusing to change. I wonder if I should phone a few customers and beg for work. But I don't. Instead, I spend my increasing free time—a benefit of the slowdown—in the backyard, journaling and gardening.

This is not how I wanted my career to end, smoldering embers instead of a blaze of glory. I try to be philosophical about the demise but I can't get there. I understand intellectually how important work is in our lives. I learned about the pain of job loss when I interviewed so many job losers for that second book. But now I'm feeling the pain. Working in a deathly quiet office each day has left me with too much time to wallow in sadness, disappointment, and frustration.

The slow death of my career, I'm sure, is part of the reason that the last year has been so emotional, has found me doubting myself, reflecting on the deaths of loved ones, questioning beliefs and decisions, and visiting my paper therapist.

Just like the fall garden, my career looks disheveled and deteriorated. I see no future, have no idea what comes next. But just as surely as spring and sprouts will come to the garden, a new season of life will arrive with retirement. I'm far too young to sit back and do nothing. This year of reflecting and writing will have helped me accept whatever lies ahead and go wherever that may lead.

CHAPTER 31

Pink Puffers

A FEW WEEKS LATER, ON THE EVE OF MY BIRTHDAY, WHEN I will turn sixty-two and officially retire, I nestle in bed next to sleeping Mary, enjoying her rhythmic breathing. I picture the next morning's reflecting and writing in the garden. To prime the pump, I pick up my journal from the bedside table, read some recent entries, and instruct my brain to ponder—while I sleep—what is important to write about on my birthday. Then I put the journal back on the table, turn out the light, spoon Mary, inhale her sweet fragrance, and drift contentedly to sleep.

In the morning after seeing Mary off to work (she still has seven demanding months before she retires), I walk to the garden and settle in. I don't have to work today or any day—the dying career has been put to rest. I have abundant time to obsess on my limited future in the wilds of aging.

I look at the blank journal page in front of me and begin free writing, wondering where my inner writer

will take me. A few lines later, I'm surprised to find
Dead Old Dad inking his way into my birthday. Seven
months ago he chided me as I shoveled rocks and clay to
enlarge the garden. Two months ago I recalled his—and
my—drinking. And now he's joining me on my birthday
and the launch of retirement. Who invited him to this
private party?

I don't know how Dead Old Dad fits into my internal
adventure. But I trust this process. I keep scribbling and
let myself join him again. Twenty-four years ago.

I glanced at the departure board and my watch yet
again. My departing flight was still on time. So was this
upcoming visit to sixty-five-year-old Dad, since he was
slowly dying in the VA hospital in Delaware.

Years of heavy cigarette smoking—especially when
he drank—had ruined his lungs, led to chronic obstruc-
tive pulmonary disease. He had bouts with COPD each
year. When breathing grew frighteningly difficult, he
would check into the VA hospital until he recovered
enough to go home. He would probably not return
home this time.

Before he died, I wanted a final—and meaningful—
conversation. At age thirty-eight, I had things I needed
to say and no idea how he might respond. On the flight
from Oregon, I tried to relax. Tried to convince myself
that his response didn't matter. But it did. A lot.

When I arrived at the hospital, I was struck by how

much more tired and frail he looked than when I last visited several months earlier. His face was thinner, the bags under his eyes bigger. His shoulders, so wide and strong and impressive when I was a kid, had narrowed and slumped.

Three days of the visit passed without our moving beyond small talk. When I walked into his room on the final morning, my stomach roiled with unasked questions. Dad was sitting up in bed, a blue-striped pajama top showing above beige covers. His red hair was, as always, oiled, neatly combed, and parted on the left.

Seeing me enter, he smiled. "Hey, Boy, how you doing?"

I walked over, hugged him, smelled his hair oil, felt the stubble of his beard. He allowed my hug but made no effort to put his arms around me. I released him and sat down. He looked out the window. I watched him breathe.

His breathing had worsened since my last visit. Now, inhaling had become more difficult; he complained that he couldn't get enough air. Exhaling was no easier: a long, slow stream of air forced through pursed lips sounded like someone blowing on a hot drink to cool it. The struggle to exhale flushed his face pink. Doctors call patients like him "pink puffers."

There was no treatment for his lungs, and they never fully recovered from each bout of COPD. They continued to inefficiently expel carbon dioxide. The buildup of carbon dioxide in his bloodstream would increase his body's acidity. Higher acidity would further damage his heart until finally his heart would stop.

I didn't know when that might happen. But I knew I had to talk with Dad now.

CHAPTER 32

Finally Spoken

DAD TURNED FROM THE HOSPITAL WINDOW AND SAID IN a voice roughened by far too many smokes, "I sure would like a cigarette."

I glared at him, hoping he was joking. His frown revealed he wasn't. "You've got to be kidding, Dad," I snapped, pointing at a pole to his left from which hung an oxygen mask attached to a portable tank. "Cigarettes are why you need to pull that thing around."

"Aw, hell," he puffed, "at least I'd die happy ... with a smoke." He puffed a pink exhale, turned his head, and gazed out the window again.

Silence.

Watching him struggle to pull air into his lungs, I struggled to speak words from my heart. This was probably the last time I would see him alive. Finally, I said the simplest thing I could think of: "I love you, Dad."

He turned toward me, a quizzical look spreading across his face. "What's that about?"

This is going to be harder than I imagined, I thought.

"I don't know how much time you have left, but I know that I have to leave today to fly home. And I don't want to leave things unsaid."

Wrinkles carved his forehead; a frown formed. "Like what?"

I squirmed in my seat, moved my head side to side, a fighter loosening up before entering the ring. Inside I debated what to do.

Maybe I should just keep my mouth shut. Hell, he'll be dead soon. What's the point?

I'll still be living and stuck with the fact that I chickened out. That's the point!

I rubbed my hands on the knees of my jeans, listened to the swishing sound. I took a deep breath, held it. Then the hurt child in me blurted, "I never understood why you made fun of me."

He slammed his head back into the pillow. His eyes darted around the room. He grabbed the oxygen mask, jammed it over his nose and mouth. Inhaled. Vapor condensed inside the mask.

I held my tongue, waiting for the response my honesty deserved.

He pulled the mask off, exhaled loudly, pointed at the bedside table, and said, "Get me some … water will you?"

I snorted through a rush of anger but reached over, poured a glass, and handed it to him. He raised it to his mouth. The glass trembled. He drank. His Adam's apple bobbed in his thin, freckled neck. He brought the half-empty glass down to rest on his chest.

Was that fear in his eyes? Had I gone too far?

Hell, no!

I leaned forward, placed my hands on the edge of the bed, felt the softness of the blankets, heard the crinkle of starched sheets. "Are you going to answer me?"

He puffed as he put the glass on the bedside table. "What makes you think ... I made fun ... of you?"

"Why do I think you made fun of me?" My voice climbed as I continued. "Oh, come on! How about the way you said I was clumsy as a bull in a china shop?"

He shrugged his shoulders, angled his head slightly. The corners of his mouth turned up.

"Or how about how you made fun of my ears?" I reached up with both forefingers and pushed my ears forward. "Like a taxi cab going down the road with its doors open. Remember that one, Dad?" I let my ears snap back.

"For Christ's sake ... those are ... just sayings, Boy."

Boy? Here I am, thirty-eight years old, a husband, a father, a successful professional, and still he calls me Boy. Won't he ever see me as grown up?

I could have caved right then. But he's dying and I've got to live with his cutting remarks, those Ben-isms that still pop into my head and belittle me, usually when I'm down or heading there.

"Those sayings hurt like hell, Dad. They still do. Couldn't you see that?" Without waiting for an answer,

I plunged ahead, fueled by anger and adrenaline. "You know the time that gets me the most?"

His eyes turned sad. He shook his head side to side.

"I was visiting you and your lady friend June. We were sitting at the dining room table and your big old German shepherd was sleeping on the living room floor. You looked at that dog and then called him. But instead of calling him by his name, Duke, you yelled, 'Rick, come here. Get over here. Now!' And he came. Then when he sat there looking at you, you smacked him on the top of the head and laughed."

"Was that all I was to you, Dad, a dog?"

A cool tear leaked onto my hot face. I brushed it off and turned away, not wanting him to see me cry, a grown man hurting like a child. I poured water into a paper cup, gulped it down as I watched the green lights of the bedside monitor.

I glanced at Dad; he was staring at me.

"I didn't know … I hurt you." His voice was between a whisper and a sob.

I sighed long and low, dropped my head to my chest. More tears welled up. I let them come. Didn't wipe them away.

"Of the three kids … you were the one … most like me … Even built like me," He pointed a trembling finger at my shoulders. "But you … could do things … I couldn't … smart in school … went to college … good with people …" He wheezed to a stop.

I looked up, speechless. *Had I ever heard him compliment me?*

Dad puffed and continued. "You were like me … Maybe better … than me … I didn't like that." He stopped, rubbed a tear from a watery blue eye, forced a breath. "Maybe that's why … I made fun … put you … in your place … feel better than you."

His confession made sense, felt true. The ridiculing wasn't about my shortcomings; it was about his insecurity.

I grabbed his hand, calloused from so many years of working with tools, knuckles thick with arthritis. "I love you, Dad."

He squeezed my hand. "I love you, too, Stud Hoss."

I inhaled a ragged breath, basking in *Stud Hoss*, the special name he called me as a kid, when he was happy. There was more to say, but I figured he had come as far as he could. And I had done what I had come to do.

We drifted into small talk and then silence. I checked my watch and saw I had to leave for the airport. I looked at him, took a deep breath, and said, "Dad, I don't believe I'll ever see you again."

He nodded, raised his right hand, waved it in dismissal. "I know that … I don't have … much time left … anyway."

I looked into his eyes, let out a long sigh. "Yeah, I know. That's why I wanted to talk with you."

I stood and bent to him. I hugged him one last time. When he hugged me back, I held on longer. Then I gently pulled away, smiled at him, and started to leave. When I reached the door of his room, I stopped, put my hand against the cool metal frame, turned, and looked back. Dad was watching me, a fog of loneliness closing in on his face. I waved and forced myself out the door.

CHAPTER 33

Not There

ON THE DAY AFTER CHRISTMAS, A COUPLE OF MONTHS after that final visit to the VA hospital, Dad died. I was not there. I wish I had been.

I can imagine him sitting on the side of his bed, bent forward, hands on knees, face red and sweating, breathing hard and fast, panic starting as he whispered to the empty hospital room, "I can't ... get enough... air."

After struggling for a while, he would close his eyes, appear to be falling asleep. But he wasn't; his body was just giving up, overwhelmed by all that was going wrong.

Scared and weak, he would hit the call button. A nurse would hustle in, look at him, and know that he was failing. She would help him lie back, tell him to relax, try to get comfortable. He would desperately want to. But he couldn't.

The nurse might wish there was more she could do, but it was just a matter of time; nothing could reverse his deadly downward spiral. The doctors wouldn't even try to resuscitate; his lungs were too far gone.

As Dad lay there, all his bodily systems would be in crisis, struggling to save his life. His heart would beat erratically, reducing the oxygen to his brain. With less oxygen, he would slip toward unconsciousness, a slow descent from light to dark, life to death. He would know that he was dying. And he would have time to think.

Did he think of the father he never really knew, of the mother who sent him and his brother as children to live with relatives?

Did he think of times in World War II, of working two jobs to support a wife and three kids?

Did he think of divorcing his wife, of smoking and drinking his life away?

Did he think of his lady friend June, his oldest son, his only daughter?

Did he think of me?

———

Sitting in the garden on my sixty-second birthday, picturing him as an old man, dying alone, I wipe away tears.

I feel guilty for not going back, not supporting him as he faced the end of his life in that hospital bed. I regret not staying in touch after that visit to the 'hospital. While he would never have written or called me, I could have reached out to him. I would have known when the end was near and he needed me.

But I think I was still too angry at his kicking Mom out, his drinking, and his indifference to being a real grandfather to my daughter. Though I don't recall thinking this then, I wonder now if I was trying to punish him by staying away.

Not only was Dad alone when he died, but he was practically alone at his funeral too. I didn't attend; neither did my brother, or Dad's older brother. There were no coworkers, no old friends. Even June didn't show. There was just a handful of people: my sister, my mother—I'm amazed she attended—and a couple of others. I'm angry at myself for not being there; he deserved at least that much.

Looking back at Dad now—after my first marriage, child rearing, divorce, current marriage, and years of helping men like him struggle through loss—I see his life in ways I couldn't imagine as a scared teenager rescuing him or as an angry adult confronting him.

As far as I know, Dad never had a parenting role model. Mom used to tell this story: Dad was home on leave from the army, early in World War II. While on leave, he and Mom had married. One day, they were walking down a street. Mom noticed Dad staring at a man who was standing in line at a movie theater. Without a word, Dad left Mom and walked to the man. They talked for a moment. Mom noticed that the man and Dad looked quite alike. Without a hug or hand-shake, Dad left the man and walked back to Mom. He took her hand and they continued down the street. Mom asked, "Who was that man?" Dad hesitated and then answered, "That was my father." He said nothing more. Mom never saw Dad and his father together again. She never told me anything else about his father.

Yes, given his upbringing, Dad did the best he could raising me. And during my last visit, he faced me—and himself—without the help of alcohol. He cried with me. As a wise person once told me, he may not have been the dad I wanted, but he is the only dad I'll ever have.

CHAPTER 34

Unlike Dad

I HAVE SPENT MY ADULT LIFE TRYING TO BE UNLIKE DAD. From the time I quit digging ditches for him; to deciding that I'd go to college to learn to work with my head instead of my hands; to becoming a manager instead of a laborer; to quitting drinking; to always trying to make sure that Allison felt loved and supported; to following my dreams wherever they took me. All of that was to be unlike Dad. Now I see there is one more way in which I can be unlike him: how I die.

This must be how Dad fits into my internal adventure. My continuing quest to be unlike him can help me plan my passing, if I'm lucky enough to have a deathbed and time before I depart.

Few people came to visit Dad in the hospital as his death approached. He passed with no loved ones in that room.

Putting myself in his place, imagining my decline and how to be unlike him, I will reach out to family and friends. Daniel showed me one way to do this, with an e-mail. I'll find something that feels right, though it may not be easy; I've never been good at reaching out. Like Dad, I don't do it naturally. But unlike him, I'll force myself if I must.

I'll ask for what I want: for loved ones to come so that we can be together again, however briefly, and hopefully in nature—a moment in the backyard, a walk, a bike ride, a spin in a wheel chair, whatever my body and mind allow. I want to look into their eyes, hold their hands, feel their warmth, hear what's in their heart. I want to tell them what I love about them, what I'll miss. I want to reminisce about times that made us laugh, cry, wonder.

There may come a time, as it did for Dad, when death is close and calling, and lying in bed is all I can do. Then, I want to be at home—unlike Dad in his hospital room.

I want the love of Mary, family, and friends to envelop me. I want to be touched. I want the windows open wide, a breeze caressing my face. I want to smell coffee and listen to those songs I worked so hard to put into LIFE MUSIC. I want to recall people, places, and times I've loved. I want to listen to the sweet sounds of redwing blackbirds, a chorus of pond frogs. If nature won't cooperate, or if the windows can't be open, then bring on the recordings. I want to sense nature, wildlife, and wild lands, to the last.

And when I'm leaving, I want each loved one to hold me and whisper final loving thoughts into my ear.

Of course, there may not be a deathbed or time to say sweet goodbyes. So I'd better write a long letter to loved ones, telling each much of what I would have said in person. That letter will be an *emotional* last will and testament to be shared after my death.

But I don't have to stash my feelings in a letter. I can make sure from this day forward to tell family and friends how much they mean, how much I love them. Then, if death takes me by surprise, my love will not be unspoken.

Yet another way I can be unlike Dad.

CHAPTER 35

Afterlife

BY MID-DECEMBER, IT'S TWENTY-EIGHT DEGREES AND THE first snow of winter covers the garden. Small flakes drift lazily down onto the inch from last night. The greens in Mammaw's Garden—arugula, Kyoto mizuna, chard, and kale—are drooping and dusted with snow. In a nearby bed, broccoli and Brussels sprouts are totally encased, no green visible.

My boots squeak on virgin snow as I walk to a bed. I kneel, pull a soil thermometer from my pocket, plunge it through snow. The bed's soil is thirty-eight degrees. I pinch off a snow-flecked arugula leaf and pop it into my mouth; it's cold and rubbery but still peppery.

I stand and start to turn a slow circle to take in the whole backyard. I stop to watch a flock of small brown birds with white chests flutter from the magnolia tree and peck in the snow, flakes flying from busy beaks. I wonder if we should start feeding birds again. The last time we tried, all we got were fat squirrels.

Under the magnolia, the ground is only dusted with snow. The tree's large thick leaves captured most of the night's snowfall; this tree does not like to share its water any time of the year. We have given up trying to grow anything in the soil beneath the magnolia; nothing can compete with its water-hungry roots. Instead, last summer we placed under the tree a collection of shade-loving plants in large pots, each on drip irrigation. They survived.

On the ends of some of the magnolia leaves, little diamonds glisten. Curious, I approach and find drops of frozen water hanging from the leaves; I can see my upside down face in some. I break off a drop, crunch it, and enjoy the chill in my throat.

I walk to a large ceramic pot filled with miner's lettuce and gently brush snow off the small delicate leaves. I taste a leaf; it's rubbery too, but still good, a bit like spinach.

I walk to the carport, grab a lawn chair, and set it in the garden. I sit down, look up at the sky, stick out my tongue, and taste snowflakes. I must look silly, tongue out, sitting in snowfall in a lawn chair meant for sunbathing. Then I hear the yelling and laughter of children sleigh riding down a nearby hilly street and I laugh out loud: fun is really in the heart and mind of the beholder.

And this internal adventure, now three-quarters over, is also in the heart and mind of the beholder, as I have discovered when telling people about my sitting in the garden and contemplating aging, death, and afterlife.

The mention of struggling with the existence of after-life often generates a response. Many people laugh—sometimes nervously—and make a quick comment like "But no one knows what happens when you die."

A few add, "That's why I'm not going to think about it till then."

Still others ask, "Would it be okay if you ended up saying that you don't know what you believe?"

I don't think it would, I tell them. There are just two possibilities: there is or is not life after death. While I concede that I'll never know in this life if I'm correct, I feel driven to be able to say, "Here's what I *believe* will happen."

Some people ignore the destination and focus on the journey by asking, "Why is deciding about afterlife so important?"

I reply that I have finally accepted that the odds are 100 percent that I'll die, and there are only a couple of ways it will happen. If I go quickly, like through a wind-shield at seventy miles per hour, I'll have little time to ponder. If I go slowly and surrounded by those I love—my preference—I will have time to think about what's next. I don't want to begin contemplating the existence of afterlife when my mind or body is failing, when I may be scared and desperate. So this is my attempt to prepare now.

And with the death of my career and the birth of retirement, I have had the time to sit and reflect, some-thing I've done precious little of in my life. Instead, I have always focused on doing and achieving. And denying, of course.

Over the past months, I've spent many hours sitting in this garden in sunshine, overcast, mist, rain, and now snow. I've reached some destinations on this unblazed trail. I've accepted aging, accompanying physical decline, and the certainty of death. I've begun preparing a memorial service to help my loved ones. I've confronted my fear of dying from Alzheimer's like Mom. I've discovered that I don't want to die alone like Dad.

Reaching each waypoint has freed me a bit more from obsessing, has made me feel more prepared for the inevitable. That's a great improvement from when I retreated to this garden, totally obsessed, completely unprepared.

But one more destination remains: to decide what I believe about life after death, to end the mind-heart debate. Is death the start of a joyous reunion and eternal bliss as Mammaw believed? Or is death just a light switch off as Daniel figured?

I feel myself drifting from Mammaw's heart and toward Daniel's mind. But I also flip-flop, sometimes in the course of a single day. This debate has evolved into a wrestling match with two well-matched, sweaty opponents, heart and mind, twisting and turning, lifting and falling, gaining and losing advantage.

There's no way to study afterlife without encountering near-death experience, a sort of proving ground in the debate between believers and nonbelievers. People who have died and come back, who have reported an

NDE, describe all sorts of experiences that believers see as proof of life after death. Nonbelievers, on the other hand, say that NDE is simply the picturesque creation of a dying brain, a scientifically explainable biological process.

While I lean in the direction of science, I also want to talk soon with Dick, a good friend. He's older than me and has had an experience I hope to never have. Perhaps he has also had an NDE.

CHAPTER 36

Flip-Flop

A FEW WEEKS LATER, I'M IN A COFFEE SHOP WITH DICK. We're seated at a table reserved for people with disabilities. A steady stream of customers snakes by our table. Some of them sneak a glance at Dick in his wheelchair, his white hair brushed back and flowing to his shirt collar.

Dick tentatively picks up a white plastic knife with the curled fingers of his right hand. He uses his more tightly curled left hand to awkwardly keep an old-fashioned donut trapped on a paper plate. He slowly moves the right hand in a tiny sawing motion, cutting the donut into smaller pieces he can grasp and lift to his mouth. I pour more coffee from a to-go cup into his blue plastic two-handled cup, the kind toddlers must use, the kind he must use.

Dick used to run marathons and swim, cycle, and run in triathlons. Life changed some years ago in a head-on collision, which he describes in his memoir,

Two Different Worlds. "Then, the shattering. Not only pieces of crushed glass, but the smashing and twisting of metal, flesh and bone, and burning. My van smashing into a cement mixer."

Rescue workers used a tool called the jaws of life to extract Dick's mangled body from his totaled van. They rushed him to the intensive care unit at the hospital in Corvallis. Once there, doctors pronounced him dead. Then he came back to life.

Though Dick has told me about his accident, I've never asked whether he had a near-death experience. He knows I'm sitting in the garden and trying to decide about life after death. He's very well read and knows of the connection between NDE and afterlife.

After Dick swallows another piece of donut, I ask. "Do you remember anything about coming back from the other side, a near-death experience?"

Dick laughs, and a crumb tumbles from his chin, snags for a moment in his gray beard, and lands on his soft, orange "Fitness Over Fifty" sweatshirt. "No, Rick, sorry, no near-death experience for me to share."

Determined, I poke and prod, hoping to uncover something. Dick recounts more of what he was told happened while he was in a coma for eight weeks.

His children—as many of the twelve as could— flocked to the ICU. His wife couldn't come. She was in an Alzheimer's fog in a memory care center. Dick was on his way to visit her when the cement truck rerouted his life.

At the hospital his children conferred with doctors,

discussing whether to pull the plug. The Corvallis doctors said they could not provide the level of care he needed for his burns; broken arms and legs; fractured hip and pelvis; and severed nerves, tendons, and ligaments. Worse yet, they didn't think he would survive the life flight to the ICU/trauma center ninety miles away in Portland.

Then Dick's family doctor intervened. "He may be seventy-two years old, but he has the body of a fifty-two-year-old."

That changed the debate. The kids rallied around their dad. The doctors agreed to risk the flight.

Dick survived the flight and multiple surgeries. He participated in years of physical therapy to return his body to the capacity it has today.

Dick can walk, but only unsteadily and for a few steps with a cane; otherwise he uses a wheelchair. His hands are permanently curled, his left of little use. He can type but must use what he calls a finger prosthetic in a process similar to one-fingered typing; that's how he wrote his memoir. He lives in an assisted living facility where aides help him with all the bodily functions he once took for granted. While his body is wrecked, his mind is sharp.

I look at Dick and feel a sense of awe. All that pain and loss and here he sits, contentedly eating a donut. I sip my coffee and wonder how he survived something that many others could not. Dick's story makes me wonder about the existence of a personal God—one that looked out for him. Finally, I ask, "What do you think helped you survive a crash that actually killed you?"

Dick looks out the window and then back to me. "The doctors told me that my body helped. I was really fit once," he says, looking with chagrin at his legs clothed in madras print cotton sweatpants, his feet in running shoes. He recalls how he used to run, bicycle, and lift weights, often at two in the morning, the only time available, since he was working three jobs—college professor, public radio program host, and co-owner of a local advertising agency—to support his huge family. "They said that the muscle I built up helped keep my body together, such as it is. And I suppose I had the will to live."

I nibble a corner of my fritter and consider what he's just said. I can surely understand that being in shape helped him survive and recover. But what's this about a will to live? "But you were unconscious at first. And then in a coma. How could your body have a will to live without consciousness?"

Dick blinks, raises his eyebrows over the upper edge of his thin-rimmed trifocal glasses. "I see where you're going."

Where I'm going is that Dick has told me in other conversations that he does not believe in afterlife and is unsure about the existence of God. He has said he takes a more scientific approach. Yet here he is, an intelligent person with a sound and logical mind, considering a will operating in an unconscious body.

"Do you think that your will is something that exists on its own? Could your doctors have given you a will transfusion, like all the blood transfusions you got?"

He chuckles, shakes his head, and looks down at the remaining half of the donut on his plate. With the back of his left hand he pushes the plate away.

Before he can answer, I continue, "It sure makes me wonder. Here I am, thinking that I don't believe in an afterlife, and wondering if there's such a thing as a personal God. Yet your survival seems magical, like someone or something was looking out for you."

He nods vigorously. "Yes, some people have told me that it wasn't my time to go." He sits silent for a moment, eyes unfocused. "I think there was a reason for not dying. I still had unfinished work. I could still teach, do some good for others, be a role model for surviving."

Dick is an agnostic, and he still thinks there was a reason he came back to life. Whose reason was it? God's? Could he believe that and be an agnostic?

My heart has no trouble believing someone or something was looking out for him. My heart is glad he's here, glad we're friends. I wouldn't have met him years ago in a writing class had he not survived. I would have missed out on our talks and our friendship.

But my mind clings to science and biology, and I say, "Maybe it was the strength of your heart and lungs and brain from all that physical and intellectual exercise before the accident. That it was as simple and as practical as that. Had you been out of shape, you might not have made it."

"That's possible. But how could anyone ever know?"

"Yeah, it always comes back to that, doesn't it?" I say. "No way to really know."

I take the last bite of my fritter, put my crumb-flecked fingertips over my heart, lean toward Dick's good ear, and say, "But I find myself struggling with this because my heart wants to believe that you had this intangible will that kept you going. A little miracle." I tap the side of my head. "But my mind says that's not logical. Can't be. That's just not a rational explanation."

"It sounds to me like you've got some more sitting in the garden to do," Dick says with a smile.

I sigh and lean back. When will this flip-flopping end?

CHAPTER 37

Student Is Ready

I'M STILL GNAWING LIKE A DOG WITH A BONE ON THE question of afterlife's existence a week after the conversation with Dick. Over breakfast I'm surprised and pleased to read in the local paper that two national experts will debate next month at nearby Oregon State University on whether—from a scientific point of view—there is life after death. How timely.

Setting the paper down, I stare unfocused at the page and think about an old saying: *When the student is ready, the teacher will come.* I become a student on life after death, and this debate appears.

My heart gushes: There's the teacher! This can't be coincidence. It must be divine intervention!

My mind reasons: It's not believable that some divine power arranged the debate, got me ready, and then directed me to the newspaper article. This is just happy coincidence.

Happy coincidence or divine intervention, I want to

prepare to meet the teachers. I want to explore how some of the major Christian religions—like those the debaters will discuss—address questions I'm grappling with. Is the body resurrected after death? Is there a heaven, and if so, is it a real place? Would I recognize friends and relatives in heaven?

I spend the next week or so preparing. I survey books on afterlife at our local library and check out a few to read in depth. Online I read summaries, reviews, and excerpts. I take lots of notes and walk away from the research a better informed—but still undecided—student. I look forward to the experts. Perhaps hearing them debate will end my flip-flopping once and for all.

On the night of the debate, I gather my notes, stride to the university, and settle my doubts into a front row seat in a rapidly filling auditorium that's abuzz with conversations and laughter. Up on stage the debaters sit, each scribbling notes and organizing papers. I glance at my watch, eager for the debate—the teaching—to begin.

To kill time, I review my notes. When looking for books at the library, I surprised myself by immediately dismissing those written by mediums and psychics who claimed to communicate with "the other side." That just didn't resonate; I have not had any communication with departed ones. The cutting remarks from Dead Old Dad reside in my memory from years of painful repetition, just waiting to assail me at the right moment. I hear those Ben-isms, but I don't believe he is sending these messages from the grave. And I sure hope he stops if we reconnect in an afterlife.

Instead, I found myself drawn to books by neuroscientists, microbiologists, and journalists writing from a more objective view (as objective as this can get) rather than a religious or philosophical perspective. I sought books that considered the medical, social, cultural, and spiritual aspects of death and life after death. My doubting, logical mind had set the ground rules for this mind-versus-heart debate.

On stage, the moderator, a young college student, steps to the lectern, introduces himself, and proclaims he's happy to see that about five hundred people have come. As he explains the ground rules of this debate and introduces the debaters, I tuck away my notes.

Dinesh D'Souza will make the case that life after death is probable from a scientific view, and that the Christian view of afterlife fits best. D'Souza is a conservative political commentator and author. He was president of Bible-based King's College in New York City, as well as a fellow at the American Enterprise Institute, a conservative think tank. His focus on a scientific view appeals to me.

Daniel Barker, on the other hand, will argue that afterlife is a popular illusion that ought to be discarded in this scientific age. He was once a pastor in the Quaker church, an Assembly of God, and a charismatic church. Now he's an atheist, author, and co-president of the Freedom From Religion Foundation, a national organization of atheists and agnostics. Barker's flip-flop intrigues me; at one time his heart believed in afterlife but now his mind does not.

What did it take for him to stop believing? What would it take for me to start?

CHAPTER 38

The Debate

D'SOUZA WINS THE COIN FLIP AND WILL PRESENT HIS view first. The audience hushes as he approaches the lectern. He clears his throat and forcefully says that he is religious and hopes for life after death. He believes that life after death is probable from a scientific point of view. He says he will show how the Christian view of afterlife best suits the evidence. Directly behind me, a father and his college-aged son mumble their approval of that stance.

D'Souza uses his hands and long fingers to punctuate other points. He peppers his talk with jokes that bring laughter from the audience and more approval from the duo behind me. My ears perk up when D'Souza says there are three conditions that have to be true for a Christian belief in life after death to be "plausible." First, heaven and hell must exist. Second, eternity must be possible. And finally, not only must the soul live on but so must the body, though not necessarily in its earthly form.

His three conditions remind me of what I learned recently after hours of studying an informative book, *How Different Religions View Death and Afterlife*. I read about the views of ten Christian religions: Assembly of God, Baptist, Church of Christ, Mormon, Lutheran, Presbyterian, Quaker, Roman Catholic, Seventh Day Adventist, and United Methodist Church. For comparison, I used other resources to dig into the views of Unitarian Universalism, the church I'm a member of.

I found that in all ten of the other religions, the body is eventually resurrected in some form. Most of those religions believe that the body is improved, even *perfected*, in the afterlife. No more diseases, deformities, or disabilities. Most Unitarian Universalists, on the other hand, see death as the end of existence.

With the ten other religions, the body resides in a heaven that's either a state of being or a place. Two of the religions describe a heaven with streets paved with gold—one even promises mansions lining glittering streets. Very few Unitarian Universalists believe in life after death. Even fewer believe in heaven or hell.

For the other ten religions, heaven will be filled with departed friends and loved ones who recognize one another. In some of these religions, the loving and living in heaven are of a wondrous quality unimaginable to a mortal. With Unitarian Universalism, of course, since our bodies do not survive death, there's nobody—no bodies—to see. It's light switch off.

I was struck most by the conviction the ten other

religions had in common: death is unavoidable, but by following a Christian lifestyle, the faithful can, in the end, beat death. As with Mammaw's view, death is not an ending; it's a beginning of a new and better life.

Listening to D'Souza expound on his three conditions, I find—as I had after reading about the ten religions—that my heart wants the reconnection with loved ones in the afterlife, but my mind doubts the existence of heaven, hell, and eternity, D'Souza's prerequisites.

But D'Souza isn't finished. He goes on to say that the ideas he presents might have seemed "kind of nuts" a hundred years ago. But he has collected new concepts from physics, biology, evolution, neuroscience, ethics, and morality that support the existence of life after death. The ideas of eternity, a resurrected body, heaven and hell are now "completely within the mainstream of modern physics," he proclaims in a loud voice. To prove this point, he rushes through a discourse of how theories of multiple universes, dark matter, and dark energy scientifically support the existence of life after death. I find his explanation hard to follow and hard to swallow.

As D'Souza concludes and walks to his seat to long and loud applause, I feel a hardening of my doubts. This surprises me since he just used science to support his view, a bandwagon my logical mind should have jumped on. But his science did not convince me.

As I watch Daniel Barker take a long drink of water, gather his notes, and step to the lectern, I wonder how he will impact my internal debate. Barker introduces himself by reminding us that he spent nineteen years preaching the gospel. He lets that sink in and then adds that while he no longer believes in God, he is not totally closed to the possibility of afterlife. But, unfortunately, he finds no real evidence of its existence.

Behind me, the father mutters, "He'll find out when Judgment Day comes, now won't he?" The son laughs. I consider moving.

Barker compliments D'Souza on his opening remarks and then dismisses them by telling us that most of what his opponent said was "hand waving." Barker begins his science-based presentation—and grabs my attention—by asking: "What is this soul that somehow survives death? Does it weigh something? Does it take up space?" He answers that many scientists now maintain that the soul is a synonym for personality or consciousness. He adds that consciousness needs a functioning brain. Then he concludes: "When the power is shut off to a functioning brain, the mind is gone. There is no mind. There is no consciousness."

I accept his reasoning and drift away for a moment as I imagine an afterlife without consciousness. Would I have senses? Could I see my loved ones, smell Mary's fragrance, hear Mom's laughter, touch Dad? Without consciousness, without senses, there would be no sense in an afterlife.

For the rest of the entertaining debate, D'Souza and Barker thrust and parry—with facts, theories, jokes, and insults—about whether near-death experiences are evidence of afterlife or the creation of a dying brain. I find myself drawn to Barker's dying-brain theory.

As the debaters wind down and the applause rises, it's clear that the father and son behind me have no doubt: D'Souza is their man.

But for me, Barker's points resonate best: there is no afterlife.

Yet my heart still lobbies for that beautiful reconnection with loved ones. That desire just won't go away.

CHAPTER 39

Leap of Faith

As I MEANDER HOME, THE EMPTY STREETS WITH ALTER-nating swaths of darkness and cones of streetlight brightness remind me of the debaters' points and counterpoints. I found D'Souza and Barker to be learned, articulate, convincing, and—of course—diametrically opposed. They had debated, as both admitted, about something that can't be objectively proved or disproved. Believing in an afterlife requires a leap of faith. D'Souza can make the leap. Barker once could; now he can't.

As I turn onto our quiet street, I again recall the beautiful afterlife that Mammaw envisioned, and I know believing in that will take a leap for me. I whisper aloud, "Can I make that leap?" I wander on in silent contemplation and then wonder: *What would drive me to do so?*

I reach our darkened house and, not wanting to disturb Mary, who must be sleeping, I sit on the front step in a shadow cast by a large blue spruce. I think about leaps of faith I saw in twenty-six years of counseling clients who, after on-the-job injuries, had lost physical abilities, jobs, and the self-esteem those jobs provided. Most of these people were middle-aged or older. While recovering from life-changing injuries, they faced returning to school, learning a new trade, and competing with younger people for jobs. They hurt physically and struggled financially. They grieved losses and feared the future.

Yet many clients overcame all that and returned to work. Over the years, I saw that their success came down to this: the heart leaps and then the mind rationalizes. People must truly want to change their situation—must desire change with their hearts and take the leap—before change occurs.

Most of the hard work I did initially with my clients was trying to help each one open up his or her heart to change, to take—on faith—that there is life after loss. Once the person believed and the heart leapt, my job was easier: I gave them information they needed to rationalize their decision and to help them succeed. But if a person didn't truly desire the change with his or her heart—did not make the leap—no amount of information or prodding from me would move them forward enough to resolve their crisis.

Like my clients when they first walked into my office, I was in full-blown crisis when I retreated to the garden. Like most of them, I felt old, vulnerable, and scared. I had suspected—as they had—that I couldn't continue on the road I had been traveling. And, just like them, I hadn't known where I was going.

During this internal adventure, my heart often longed to leap, to believe in life after death. Even tonight while my mind rejected most of D'Souza's arguments and accepted Barker's, my heart kept pushing. With just one leap, I could accept that after death I would not only live again, but do so with those I love. I could accept death and beat it! My heart yearned to leap, while my mind—as it has done so often—resisted.

Now, after all the time in the garden, after all I've read, seen, heard, or thought, nothing enables me to make the leap. Instead, I accept that the life I have now is the only one I'll ever have.

When Daniel first shared the light switch–off concept, I felt it was an empty ending. And maybe it is. But now I see that dismissing an afterlife can help me delight in this life. Every minute with Mary, my family, and friends can feel more precious because there are no other moments waiting in an endless, perfect afterlife. As Daniel wrote in his e-mail asking us to be his Sherpas, "Let's make the most of the time that we get to share together."

Today is all I have.

CHAPTER 40

Cold Frame

I KNEEL BESIDE THE COLD FRAME, MY JOURNAL IN HAND.
My breath creates a vapor trail in twenty-seven-degree
air on this second day of February. I try to ignore the
chill nipping at my knee through two layers of fleece.

This cold frame, a simple wooden structure I built
and covered with thick plastic that has aged from clear
to translucent, has a slanted lid aimed at the sun's souther-
ly path. Because of the cold temperatures, I have kept
the lid closed. Some of yesterday's condensation clung
to the inside of the lid and froze.

I raise the lid, prop it open, and run my gloved finger
over the ice, rough to the touch, like goose bumps. I
look at the plants inside the cold frame: arugula, Kyoto
mizuna, corn salad. All droop in the below-freezing
temperature. I push on several and find each stiff, ice-
like. If I hadn't seen these plants recover from other
freezes, I'd swear they were dead.

But this cold frame, a perfect winter microclimate,

provides everything plants need for survival and growth. The closed cold frame captures the sun's light and warmth, blocks the wind's chill. Evaporation from the plants rises skyward, hits the plastic ceiling, collects into drops, and falls to the ground, watering the very plants that produced the moisture.

My backyard retreat has been my cold frame for the last year. Its top: the ever-changing sky. Its walls: the tall arborvitae, the ten-foot high wall of ivy, and the back of our house. My cold frame kept the world out, allowed me to focus on and journal about aging, declining, death, and afterlife.

The stories I recalled of external adventures were like the life-sustaining evaporation produced by the cold frame's plants. The stories rose from my memory and then rained down on me, offering lessons from "out there" that would help me grow "in here."

The months of reflecting and journaling, the adventure lessons, and the beginning of retirement came together to create a perfect microcosm for exploring the wilds of aging. Though I didn't know it at first, this little garden retreat held everything I needed.

Now, as the winter sun starts rising over our house, I watch transfixed as a horizontal swath of sunlight creeps forward from the cold frame's rear wall, like the light of a copy machine moving under its glass in slow motion. As the sunlight reaches a frozen plant, the plant twitches, shakes, shudders, and stands a little taller.

I doubt what I see and wonder if the shuddering is

from drops of melting ice falling onto the plants from the propped-open roof. To find out, I rip an empty page from my journal and lay it over the top of several twitching plants. I hold my breath, waiting to see if dripping water will spot the page. It doesn't.

Amazed, I let out a long breath and force myself to stay still and observe. The pattern repeats: as each plant receives the sun's blessing, it shakes out of the night's suspended animation. As sunlight fills the cold frame's interior, the twitching increases, plants randomly shuddering, a scene in time lapse photography. Though I don't understand the science of this, I am awed.

But why am I surprised to see plants responding to the sun? Sitting here, I feel my body loosen and relax as the sun warms me through winter clothing. Am I any different from these plants?

The sun's rays now melt in earnest the ice on the inside of the cold frame's top. Drops thaw, calve, and slide down the ice-covered plastic. A tiny sun twinkles in each drop as it moves over the rough surface. Drops marry others, growing larger, making a scraping sound as they slide downward, until they break free and plummet. Some land on plants, shattering into droplets that glitter on leaves. As the sun heats the top, more rivulets form, creating a noisy rain shower of ice melt.

When I planted in the cold frame last September, I didn't know if the plants would ever be ready for harvest, or even survive. Much to my surprise they have done both.

When I planted myself in the garden, I didn't know if I would adventure again. Now I know I will. But having accepted my mortality and that there is no limitless time horizon, I now accept that each adventure can be the last. And as my body ages and I decrease the physical challenge of the adventures, each will be different. So be it.

However much time I have left on this earth, it's up to me to make the most of it. Mary will retire in just a few months, and then we'll be free to create a new life together, to journey together into the wilds of aging.

We have just started talking about volunteering and living in Yellowstone—a place we love and want to learn more about.

I am ready for adventure.

Afterword

Years have passed since that life-changing summer that began with the exhausting bike tour in the North Cascades and drove me to sit for a year in the garden.

As I came to realize during that year, I still believe that today is all I have. I often—though not always—see each day as a gift. Of course, living in Gardiner, at the north entrance of Yellowstone, helps. We are surrounded by mountains and bluebird skies, visited by elk and bison, and serenaded by wolves and coyotes.

I've had no memory issues—other than those I consider normal for a person turning seventy. In fact, I sometimes feel that all the reading and writing I now do helps keep my mind and memory healthy.

My body has stayed healthy too. Depending on the season, Mary and I hike, bike, canoe, or cross-country ski several times a week. We explore Yellowstone and the wild lands of the West. Though I'm fit and adventuring, there's no denying that I'm older; what was once a warm-up is now a workout. I accept this decline that has come with aging—while doing what I can to minimize it.

I have not completed the planning of my memorial service, and that bothers me. I still have images to gather, words to write. I still need to write a long letter to loved ones, an emotional last will and testament. I will face these challenges. Reliving this adventure of mind and heart has helped me prepare to meet my bear again.

While sitting in the garden, I wondered if I would suffer for the rest of my life from Dead Old Dad's Ben-isms. Recently I had to dig several large holes to plant trees in our Gardiner front yard. The soil was rocky, and just as on that day so long ago, I fought with rocks bigger than the shovel blade. But I got those rocks out and never heard a snide remark from Dad. That yearlong visit to my paper therapist must have helped.

I no longer obsess on death, but I'm glad I did during the year in the garden. All that reflecting and writing opened me up to the pull of Yellowstone, and I'm thankful that Mary and I accepted that pull. Doing so gave my heart and mind something to treasure in this final phase of my life: an exciting journey as a writer and advocate for wildlife and wild lands.

A Message to the Reader

Dear Reader,

I chose to self-publish this book because I wanted more control over the finished work. But self-publishing means that I don't have the muscle of a traditional publisher to promote the book. There's just me. And you, the satisfied reader.

You can help me—and other indie authors—by taking a moment to click onto Amazon.com and rate this book. Your star rating and review (no matter how brief) helps other readers find books by indie authors.

Thanks for reading and helping,

Rick

I welcome friends, followers, and connections on social media including:
Blog: ricklamplugh.blogspot.com
Facebook: Rick Lamplugh
LinkedIn: Rick Lamplugh
Google+: Rick Lamplugh
Vimeo: vimeo.com/ricklamplugh

About the Author

Rick Lamplugh lives in Gardiner, Montana, at Yellowstone's north gate. He writes to protect wildlife and preserve wild lands.

His last book, *Deep into Yellowstone: A Year's Immersion in Grandeur and Controversy*, won a Gold Medal in the Independent Publisher Book Awards (IPPY Awards). It was a finalist in the Next Generation Indie Book Awards and in the National Indie Excellence Awards. It won an Honorable Mention in the Eric Hoffer Book Awards and in the INDIES Book Awards.

In *Deep into Yellowstone*, Rick captures the grandeur of Yellowstone while digging into important controversies: the outrage over the removal of grizzlies from the endangered species list; the dispute over hunting park wolves along Yellowstone's border; the debate about whether wolves help or harm the ecosystem and the economy; the fight to stop the slaughter of park bison; the overuse of the park; and the battle to prevent gold mining on the park's border.

His earlier book, *In the Temple of Wolves: A Winter's Immersion in Wild Yellowstone*, is an Amazon best seller with more than three hundred Five-Star reviews. The book is about the wolves and ecology of Yellowstone's

Lamar Valley and Rick's life-changing experience of living and volunteering there for three winters.

Rick's stories have appeared in *Yellowstone Reports* and the literary journals *Composite Arts Magazine, Gold Man Review, Phoebe, Soundings Review,* and *Feathered Flounder.* He won the Jim Stone Grand Prize for Non-Fiction.

Acknowledgments

Though sitting in the garden for a year while wandering in the wilds of aging was a solo internal adventure, publishing this book is a team effort. As an indie author, I have to create the team that launches a book. I've been fortunate to have found wonderful team mates.

Once I thought I was finished writing *The Wilds of Aging*, I sent it to my two editors. First was C. Lill Ahrens, who also edited my last two books. She is a "story editor" and made sure that I told each and every story in the best way possible. Any praise I receive for storytelling is due in large part to Lill. After I made the changes Lill suggested and again thought I was finished, I sent the book to its second editor, Sheridan McCarthy of Meadowlark Publishing Services. She edited the text to make my writing as grammatically correct and clear as possible. Her skill and attention to detail greatly improved this book. I give Lill and Sheridan my deepest thanks and highly recommend both of these editors to any indie author.

While the editors worked on the words, Jamie Tipton of Open Heart Designs did wonders with the design of the cover and interior. She made the book visually appealing and easier to read. Jamie is a pleasure to work with and I recommend her to any indie author.

After I made the changes the editors suggested, I sent the manuscript off to prepublication reviewers. These fine folks took the time to read the book, write comments, and compose a blurb. That gift of time and attention is so special in today's busy world. Many thanks to Lorraine Anderson, Marc Beaudin, Jenny Golding, Caroline Kraus, Ann McQueen, Lori Smetanka, Mary Reynolds Thompson, Tom Titus, Stephen Trimble, and Dick Weinman.

Of course, this book would never have come to life without wonderful moments with Jana, Daniel, Misty, and Mammaw. I thank each for sharing a part of their life and their passing with me. I thank my sister, Judy, brother, Rus, and sister-in-law Faith for listening to me read the parts of this book related to Mom and Dad and for sharing heartfelt comments, suggestions, and support. Thanks go to my sister-in-law Janet and brother-in-law Al for reading the parts of this book related to Mammaw and providing loving comments and support. Thanks also to my friend Jim for allowing me to share stories from our bicycling adventures.

Finally, and always, my deepest thanks to Mary. She read, or listened to me read, each chapter multiple times. She gave feedback even when she knew I might not want to hear it. She encouraged me to keep going with this book when I found myself backing away. I love having Mary as my partner in our journey into the wilds of aging.

An Excerpt from

Deep into Yellowstone: A Year's Immersion in Grandeur and Controversy

CHAPTER 1:

Wild Wolves in Action

As mary and i drive toward home, tired and happy from a day of cross-country skiing, we enjoy the warm touch of low, western sun streaming through our car windows. The view beyond those windows is grand, northeastern Yellowstone at its best. The two-lane, snow-covered road snakes along the side of a narrow canyon cut by Soda Butte Creek. Two mountains crowd either side, both over 10,000 feet high, one draped with an abundance of frozen waterfalls.

Gradually, the canyon widens and we slow and scan for moose as we pass by Round Prairie. Moments later the sulfur scent of Soda Butte Cone—an ancient thermal feature—floats to us on the air from the car's heat vents. Further on, we pass a ridge where Bighorn sheep rest in the sun.

Rounding a curve, we enter our favorite part of Yellowstone National Park, the Lamar Valley. We lived in the heart of this wildlife-filled valley for three winters when we volunteered at the Lamar Buffalo Ranch. Those wild winters changed our lives, led us to leave Corvallis, Oregon, our home for thirty-five years, where we had raised our kids and crafted our careers. We moved to Gardiner, Montana, right next door to Yellowstone.

As we near the entrance road to the Buffalo Ranch, we see a swarm of cars crammed into a pullout.

"What do we have here?" Mary asks as she slows the car.

"I wonder if the Mollie's are here again today," I reply. The Mollie's, one of Yellowstone's wolf packs, lives most of the year in another valley south of here. But they swagger into the Lamar Valley each winter in search of prey. We heard yesterday that they have arrived.

After a day of skiing in silent splendor, neither of us is keen on being engulfed by a crowd, but the possibility of seeing those beautiful wolves in their healthy pack lures us in. Mary maneuvers into the last available spot and cuts the engine.

Outside we hear the excited chatter of some of the many visitors here for January's long Martin Luther King Jr. weekend. Some peer into spotting scopes trained on the base of Specimen Ridge, more than a mile away, across the valley floor. Located between us and the ridge, the Lamar River hides under ice and snow. A few of the Lamar Valley's often-photographed cottonwoods reveal its frozen, winding path.

"Hmm, let's see what's happening," Mary says. She reaches into the glove box for binoculars, brings them to her eyes, and focuses. Mary's vision is much better than mine; she has what I call guide eyes. I sit and wait for her to learn why everyone is here so late in the day.

"Holy smokes! It is the Mollie's!" she exclaims, amazement in her voice.

Thrilled, I gauge the general direction of her discovery, grab my camera and, using the telephoto lens like binoculars, zoom in on the pack, mostly black wolves and a few grays. They crouch, tails down, one behind the other, forming a long line that points west. I pan in the direction they stare and soon a group of about twenty bison, big adults, mid-sized yearlings, and smaller calves, fills my viewfinder. "Whoa! We're going to see them hunt bison!"

I can't believe our luck. The Mollie's are the only Yellowstone wolves that regularly take down adult bison. And we've never seen them do so. Few people have.

Mary tosses the binos onto the dashboard, jumps out of the car, and reaches into the backseat to grab her spotting scope.

As she hustles to the edge of the knee-high snow berm that lines the pullout and the road, I step out to watch the pack through the viewfinder. They start moving: first in a walk, then a trot, then a lope. "They're running!" I shout to Mary. As I swing the camera to the west, I say in a softer voice, "And so are the bison!"

"Oh, I'll never get this thing set up in time," Mary mutters, wrestling with the legs of the tripod.

"Take your time," I tell her. "This could last a while."

Once the tripod is stable, she'll attach her iPhone to the spotting scope, which will then function as a telephoto lens to pull the action in closer than I can with my handheld camera. I assume she'll video; I know I will. By studying our footage, we'll learn more about how wolves and bison interact in this rarely seen confrontation. We'll share the footage with friends—some are Yellowstone guides and instructors—and hear what they have to say. The chance to observe and learn like this is one of the reasons we moved here.

In the viewfinder, I follow the chase: the bison, running, tails up, bodies rocking up and down with their stiff-legged gait; the wolves, tails straight out, bodies arching and flowing as their legs fully extend to the front and rear. Then one of the winter-naked cottonwoods comes between me and the wolves, blocking my view. Damn! I grunt and yank the camera from my eye.

These wolves that fascinate us, these Mollie's, once called the Lamar Valley home. The pack—one of the first released during the controversial wolf reintroduction in 1995—was then named the Crystal Creek pack. While they denned near this location in the spring of 1996, the just-released Druid Peak pack attacked and killed the Crystal Creek's alpha male and every pup. The two surviving Crystal Creek wolves, the alpha female and a male, fled to Pelican Valley, about twenty miles south. The two denned the next year and produced a litter of six pups. Their pack grew and in 2000 was renamed to honor Mollie Beattie, the late director of the US Fish & Wildlife Service, who had been instrumental in returning wolves to Yellowstone. This year the pack contains sixteen wolves; six more than the average for park packs.

I look farther west and spot a place where I think I can video without being blocked by cottonwoods. I glance over at Mary; she has the scope set up and wears a frown of concentration as she wiggles the iPhone onto the eyepiece. Not wanting to disturb her, I leave the pullout without a word. I walk by parked cars, past other excited watchers standing at silent scopes and clicking cameras, and onto the edge of the road. In the distance, the wolves and bison are still running. And now, so am I.

A few hundred yards later I step off the road and sink to my knees into the snow berm. The snow chills through my socks, and I realize that I am in low-cut shoes. In my rush to action, I neglected to put on the insulated boots that sit warm and dry in the car. I look back at the car, down at my snow-covered feet, and out at the wolves. No question: Wild wolves take precedence over warm feet. I raise the camera back to my eye. The Mollie's have sprinted past the bison they first chased and are near another group of about twenty adults, yearlings, and calves. The viewfinder scene rises and falls with my breathing, ragged after jogging at 6,600 feet of elevation. I chant aloud to myself, "Slow down. Breathe. Relax." I stabilize and so does the image. I push the RECORD button and settle into the thrill of capturing this spectacle.

The bison have raised their tails. That tail—short with long strands of fur at the tip—is a flag that denotes danger. The higher that flag, the more agitated the bison. As the old saying goes: a raised tail means charge or discharge. Now most of those tails are straight up, as high as they can go. I'm thinking charge.

The bison start to run en masse. As they gallop in

an elongated cluster through snow that almost brushes their underbellies, their hooves kick up a low white fog that hangs in the air behind them. Some of the Mollie's run just behind the group, disappearing and reappearing in the fog. Other wolves lope beside the group, which has no stragglers and little space between the animals. If a careless wolf breached that group, it could be kicked, trampled, or gored. But the Mollie's know what they're doing. These experienced hunters are sorting and sifting, looking and listening and smelling for anything out of the ordinary, any sign that reveals a vulnerable bison, a possible meal.

Bison are part of, but not all of, this pack's diet. Their menu varies, depending on the time of year and location of their prey. From June through early November when elk roam the Mollie's Pelican Valley home, up to 80 percent of the pack's diet is elk. Once winter arrives and elk leave Pelican Valley, the pack has two options, according to a Yellowstone Wolf Project annual report. (The Wolf Project brought the wolves to Yellowstone from Canada and continues to study them.)

Their first option is to follow the elk. That's why the Mollie's return to the elk-heavy Lamar Valley each winter. They stay longer some years as opposed to others. One year, when they were the largest pack in Yellowstone, they lingered here for much of winter and spring.

Their second option is to stay in Pelican Valley and switch to eating bison. Bringing down a bison—an animal ten to fifteen times heavier than a wolf and armed with sharp horns and deadly hooves—is more dangerous than bringing down an elk and may take days. To improve their odds of success, the pack, as they are doing now, seeks vulnerability. Bison are most vulnerable during winter, and from January through April, bison make up at least 80 percent of the Mollie's diet.

When the Mollie's hunt bison during the winter in Pelican Valley, the area is not accessible by car. That's why so few people have witnessed these wolves take a bison. Could we be lucky enough to see them bring down one today in the Lamar Valley?

The chase continues away from where I stand and dwindles in my viewfinder. I trudge through deep snow back to the road. Once there, I trot in the direction the animals are running. There are no cars moving in either lane, but four cars, flashers blinking, windows down, and optics protruding have turned one lane of this public road into an illegal parking lot. I jog past the stationary vehicles and keep running until I'm out of breath. Luckily, I have reached a spot with an unobstructed view. I step off the road, look into the camera, again slow my breathing, and start recording.

Behind me, I hear tires crunch to a stop on the snow-covered road. Then Mary's excited voice: "Oh, there you are. I wondered where you'd gone." She chuckles. "Is this incredible or what?"

"I can't believe we're seeing this," I say, my eye still at the viewfinder.

"What are you going to do?" she asks.

"I'm going to stay here for a while and video. Why don't you go on to the next pullout?"

As Mary drives away, I smile, pleased by our shared focus on catching every possible moment of this wild action.

The bison stop running and tighten their formation. Their collective breath creates a cloud above their massive backs. The closest wolves stop too, awaiting other pack members. As the wolves arrive, they greet each other with a lick or a bump.

As hunters and hunted catch their breath, I look down the road for *my* packmate. Mary's probably at that next pullout, about three-quarters of a mile away. Joining her would put me closer to this scene and provide a better viewing angle. I start jogging again, passing more vehicles idling in the road. At the head of another illegal line, a man and woman have climbed out of their truck. She is setting up a spotting scope in the middle of the lane between her truck and the car parked behind it. I slow to a walk and duck my head as I pass in front of her scope.

When I glance again at the wolves, I see they have now encircled the group of bison; the next act in nature's play is about to begin. I pick up my pace and my panting. As I close in on the packed pullout, I spot our car but not Mary. I'm not surprised that she has sought a private place away from the crowd. Now I just have to find her. I jog past the pullout and there she is in her perfect spot:

alone, well off the road, hunched over her scope in snow almost to her knees.

When I reach her, she flashes that smile I love: the I'm-so-excited-I-can-hardly-stand-it one. While Mary has a wonderful smile any time of year, this rendition usually appears only in Yellowstone. Then she points to her iPhone, signals me to silence, and returns to videoing. I move a few feet away, tramp a circle in the snow, squat, and rest my left elbow on my left knee to steady the camera. I put eye to the viewfinder and focus on the unfolding drama.

The bison have crowded together, big heads and sharp horns pointing outward, forming a prickly perimeter. The wolves stand nearby, panting and peering at the bison and one another. The standoff continues until a large female bison steps away from her group and toward four wolves. Three wolves immediately back away, but one stands its ground. The bison approaches until predator and prey are inches apart, noses nearly touching. Is she testing the wolves in the same way the wolves are testing the bison? The two stand statue-still, eyes locked. Who will blink first?

The wolf's mouth opens and closes, and a moment later the tough predator tucks its tail and backs away. With no hesitation, the bison takes four steps forward, head down, horns at the ready. Then, as if on cue, she and the wolf stop. The testing is over; neither animal will waste any more of the energy that's in such scant supply during winter.

Meanwhile, at the other end of the group, six black wolves and two grays have separated and surrounded another big female bison. She wears a leather collar that has a small white box attached to it. The box contains electronics that transmit data park biologists use to determine where bison roam.

But right now that white box broadcasts her mood to the wolves as it moves up and down with the aggressive bobbing of her head. The bison charges a gray wolf and then the half-ton ballerina spins to face two oncoming blacks. High-pitched wolf howls drift in from the east, a surreal soundtrack to this deadly dance.

"Oh my God," Mary whispers in awe. "This could be it."

I don't reply; I'm too engrossed watching the collared bison spin this way and that, keeping the wolves at bay. Yet despite all this dancing, I don't see the wolves biting, the bison goring or kicking.

The rest of the bison come to the collared female's aid. They surround her, snorting clouds of breath and kicking sprays of snow at the wolves. The hunters retreat to a safe distance. This is another way in which hunting bison is more dangerous than hunting elk. In an elk herd chased by wolves, it's every animal for itself. Not so with bison; these animals protect their own.

The bison continue lunging at the wolves. Finally, one by one, the wolves back off. Heads down, following in each other's steps, the predators climb a nearby slope. All that is except one, which has yet to disengage. The holdout walks through the group until a bison charges and chases. Then the lone wolf scoots for the safety of the pack. The bison, tails now down, watch the pack retreat.

At the top of the snow-covered rise, the Mollie's stop in a long, beautiful line, heads up, ears alert. They appear to be awaiting an order. Then the pack moves single file down the far side of the hill and out of our sight.

Mary and I step away from the optics, grin at each other and tap gloved knuckles. As we pack our gear and head for the car, we don't know whether the Mollie's have given up or whether their reconnaissance was productive and they will return with darkness, hungry and ready for the hard work of making dinner.

What we do know is that we were afforded a rare gift to have watched these wild wolves in action.

Made in the USA
Monee, IL
02 September 2019